CHOCOLATE

CHOCOLATE

HEAVENLY RECIPES FOR DESSERTS, CAKES AND OTHER DIVINE TREATS

JENNIFER DONOVAN

DUNCAN BAIRD PUBLISHERS

LONDON

Chocolate
Jennifer Donovan

First published in the UK and USA
in 2013 by Duncan Baird Publishers,
an imprint of Watkins Publishing Limited
Sixth Floor
75 Wells Street
London W1T 3QH

A member of Osprey Group

Osprey Publishing Inc.
43-01 21st Street
Suite 220B, Long Island City
New York 11101

Recipes taken from *The Big Book of Chocolate*,
first published in 2008 by DBP.

For my family: Kevin, Chris and James

Commissioning Editor: Grace Cheetham
Managing Editor: Sarah Epton
Editors: Alison Bolus, Judith More
Managing Designer: Manisha Patel
Design: Gail Jones
Photography: William Lingwood
Food Stylists: Bridget Sargeson, Jayne Cross
Prop Stylists: Helen Trent, Lucy Harvey

ISBN: 978-1-84899-118-7

10 9 8 7 6 5 4 3 2 1

Typeset in Goudy Old Style
Color reproduction by PDQ, UK
Printed in China

Publisher's note: While every care has been
taken in compiling the recipes for this book,
Watkins Publishing Limited, or any other
persons who have been involved in working on
this publication, cannot accept responsibility
for any errors or omissions, inadvertent or
not, that may be found in the recipes or text,
nor for any problems that may arise as a result
of preparing one of these recipes. If you are
pregnant or breastfeeding or have any special
dietary requirements or medical conditions, it
is advisable to consult a medical professional
before following any of the recipes contained
in this book.

UNLESS OTHERWISE STATED:
• Use extra large eggs
• Do not mix metric and imperial measurements
• 1 tsp. = 5ml • 1 tbsp. = 15ml • 1 cup = 240ml
• All recipes serve 4

Contents

Introduction

There are few things in the world that evoke such intense emotions as chocolate. Silky, smooth, and sensuous, chocolate has been around for centuries. It is thought to have been discovered in Mexico by the Aztec Indians and then brought to Spain in the 16th century. It is believed that the Aztec Indians first used beans from the cacao tree to make a drink for royal occasions, and that the Spaniards made this bitter drink more palatable by adding cane sugar and spices such as cinnamon and vanilla. By the 17th century, drinking chocolate was fashionable throughout Europe; and by the 19th century, chocolate to eat had been developed, and traditional hand-manufacturing methods for making chocolates gave way to mass production.

Today, chocolate has become more popular than ever. Gourmet chocolate boutiques cater for the growing passion for top-quality chocolate. Around the world, consumers are demanding better-sourced and higher-quality ingredients, so fair trade chocolate (where the cocoa beans have been sourced directly from farmers at prices that allow the farming communities to thrive and expand) and organic chocolate are both reaching a wider market.

This comprehensive book explains all you need to know about chocolate. It guides the home cook through a range of delicious chocolate recipes, from fabulous homemade cakes, brownies, ice creams, puddings, and muffins to spectacular desserts and handmade chocolates. Some of them will be familiar favorites, while others will provide some new and exciting ways to use chocolate.

As well as providing a wealth of simple-to-follow recipes and briefly outlining the origins of chocolate, this book explains in simple terms the most common ingredients and methods used when cooking with chocolate—all designed to make the recipes even easier for you to reproduce at home.

WHAT IS CHOCOLATE?

Cocoa beans, from which chocolate is derived, are a product of the cacao tree. This is believed to have originated in the tropical areas of South America, although the exact location is a source of some dispute. A relatively delicate plant, the cacao tree needs protection from wind and a good amount of shade; it usually bears fruit in the fifth year of cultivation in natural conditions. Although there are about 20 different varieties of cacao plant, only three are widely used in the making of chocolate—Forastero, Crillo, and Trinitero.

The fruit of the cacao plant, known as "pods," contain between 20 and 50 cream-colored beans, and it takes about 400 beans to make just one pound of chocolate. The beans are fermented, dried, cleaned, and roasted. Then the roasted beans are ground to produce a thick cacao liquor, or cacao mass, and finally pressed to extract the fat, known as cocoa butter.

Cacao liquor and cocoa butter are the essential ingredients in any chocolate product, and the amount included varies from around 25 percent of the product's weight up to approximately 80 percent, occasionally more. Other ingredients, including sugar, vanilla, and milk, are added to the chocolate before it goes through the final processing stages. Generally, the sweeter the chocolate, the more sugar has been added and the less cacao liquor and cocoa butter it contains. The darker and more bitter the chocolate, the higher the cacao liquor and cocoa butter content; this is widely considered to be a superior chocolate. However, chocolate preferences vary between individuals, so it is best to experiment with what you have available to see which you prefer.

TYPES OF CHOCOLATE

There are a number of basic categories of chocolate. The first is dark chocolate, sometimes referred to as bittersweet or semi-sweet chocolate, or couverture. This is designed for both eating and cooking. Look for chocolate with a high cocoa content (usually marked as a percentage on the label). Ideally, the percentage should be somewhere between 70 and 85 percent, although it is important to remember what you are ultimately using it for. The most readily available chocolate tends to range between 60 and 70 percent, which renders good results, though higher percentages do exist.

The recipes in this book have all been made with dark chocolate (where specified) with a cocoa butter content of 70 percent. However, if you want to enjoy the best-quality chocolate straight from the packet, be aware that many people prefer the highest cocoa butter content they can find, which can be up to about 85 percent. I prefer not to use a chocolate of that percentage for cooking because the result can often be too bitter for a chocolate sauce or cake, which requires a slightly sweeter finish.

Milk chocolate, which is also commonly available, generally contains less than 3 percent cocoa butter and has sugar, milk powder, and vanilla added. It is not as successful in baking and cooking as dark chocolate, but you can still use it as a substitute in mousses, fillings, drinks, and cookies, particularly if they are destined for young children, who prefer the less bitter flavor of milk chocolate. Again, for the tastiest results, look for good-quality milk chocolate—many manufacturers use vegetable oils, artificial flavors, fillers, and milk solids in their products. Organic varieties of chocolate are a good choice here.

White chocolate, another widely available product, is technically not chocolate at all because it does not contain cacao liquor—it is made from cocoa butter, sugar, milk, and vanilla. Although not a pure chocolate, white chocolate is still very popular and gives good results in cooking.

Cocoa powder and chocolate drink mixes are also derived from chocolate. "Dutch-processed" cocoa, where the cocoa is treated with an alkali to give a slightly different flavor and a darker appearance, is considered to have the best taste. Cocoa powder is derived from the pressed cake that remains after most of the cocoa butter has been removed. It may have 10 percent or more cocoa butter content. Most commercial chocolate drink mixes (which are designed to be made into hot or cold drinks) are usually made from a mixture of cocoa powder and sugar. Both cocoa powder and chocolate drink mixes have their uses in cooking, but, as with chocolate, the quality does vary, so experiment with the different brands and buy the best you can afford.

STORING CHOCOLATE

As a rough guide, chocolate will keep for a year if stored in the correct conditions. Store in a cool place—around 70°F—and don't refrigerate it unless the temperature is very hot because the moist environment of the refrigerator will shorten the life of the chocolate. Chocolate also absorbs the odors of foods stored around it, so be sure to keep it wrapped tightly in plastic wrap or in a container with a tight-fitting lid.

The white film sometimes found on chocolate that has been stored incorrectly is called a "bloom." This is caused by condensation that has melted the surface sugar on the chocolate, and, although it will not taste or look as nice as chocolate in good condition, it can still be used for melting or baking.

COOK'S INGREDIENTS

Most of the ingredients used in this book are widely available and are often very standard, but it is worth noting a few specific points.

Butter—all recipes, unless otherwise stated, use salted butter.

Eggs—extra-large eggs are used in all the recipes. Some recipes contain raw eggs, which carry a slight risk of salmonella, and should therefore be served with care and not be given to small children, pregnant women, or the elderly.

Flour—all-purpose flour and self-rising flour are used throughout this book. If you do not have any self-rising flour and need to make some, simply add 1½ tsp. baking powder and ½ tsp. salt to every 1 cup all-purpose flour.

Gold leaf—this is an edible product and is most commonly available from specialist cake-decorating suppliers.

Gelatin—Leaf gelatin comes in solid sheets that you soak in cold water until they soften. They then dissolve easily in very warm liquid. You can buy powdered gelatin, which is usually sold in ¼oz. envelopes; one envelope will set about 2 cups liquid.

Sugar—superfine sugar is used predominantly in the Baking chapter because its fine-grained quality gives the best results. However, you can substitute regular granulated sugar for superfine cup for cup.

COOK'S TOOLS

You will not need much specialist equipment when working with chocolate. The recipes in this book use a standard range of kitchen utensils, including loose-bottomed springform cake pans and fluted tart pans in a variety of shapes and sizes. However, some items you may not already have do make the process that much easier.

Baking beans—these are ceramic beads used to weigh down a pastry shell when baked "blind," that is, without a filling.

Baking paper (sometimes called baking parchment)—this is used for lining pans and baking sheets.

Double boiler—this consists of a saucepan fitted with a smaller pan on top. The bottom pan holds water, which is heated, while the ingredients sit in the top, away from direct contact with the heat. It is useful for heating and melting delicate ingredients, such as chocolate and egg custards.

Electric hand mixer—this will enable you to beat and whisk ingredients with minimum effort. Alternatively, use a hand whisk or electric stand mixer (where applicable).

Food processor—use this to crush biscuits for crumb crusts and to bind cookie dough, among other culinary jobs.

Baking sheets and pans—use nonstick bakeware when possible, ideally silicone, which is durable and flexible. Note that cake and flan pans come in various depths, and it is important to use the recommended depth to avoid having too much or too little filling. Choose pans with loose bottoms for ease.

COOKING TECHNIQUES

Using a bain marie—this French cookery term refers to a "water bath." You use this method to cook food in the oven very gently (often fragile dishes such as baked custards) and to prevent overcooking. You place the dish in which the food is cooked inside a larger vessel (sometimes with a cloth underneath to protect the base), which you then fill with water to come half way up the dish.

Melting chocolate—chocolate is a delicate product and can burn easily. It melts best at temperatures between 104°F and 113°F. A double boiler is effective (see above) and prevents the chocolate from overheating, but you can also melt chocolate in a single saucepan directly on the stove over a very low heat, as long as you watch it closely and stir it gently. Alternatively, you can use a microwave oven. The time needed will vary depending on the amount of chocolate being melted and the power of the microwave, so it's best to experiment to find out what works best for you. As a guide, use 30-second bursts until the chocolate is melted, stirring gently in between.

Tempering—this process involves heating and cooling chocolate at specific temperatures. It stabilizes the chocolate and gives it a shiny appearance as well as a hard texture. Tempering is mainly used by professional chocolate makers and can be done by hand or by machine. This process is not necessary for the recipes in this book.

FINISHING TOUCHES

Chocolate curls, leaves, and piped shapes are simple to make and add a special touch to the final product.

Making chocolate curls—a simple way is to sweep a wide-bladed vegetable peeler over a block of chocolate. Keep the chocolate cool, or the curls will loose their shape. A slightly more complicated way is to spread melted chocolate over a marble slab, if you have one, or the back of a large metal baking sheet. Leave to cool and then slide a long-bladed knife along the surface of the chocolate to create a curl. This can take a little practice but is very rewarding. You can use this technique with dark, milk, or white chocolate, or a combination of two or more, which can look quite impressive.

Making chocolate leaves—simply brush melted chocolate on the back of a clean, well-defined leaf and chill. When cold, simply peel off the leaf, leaving a delicate imprint of veins on the chocolate.

Piping chocolate shapes and lines—you can pipe chocolate shapes with a fine nozzle onto baking paper—but don't make them too delicate or they will fall apart. Chill, then lift off as required. You can also randomly pipe lines of dark and white chocolate quite densely over baking paper, then set aside to chill and break off pieces as required. This is a simple and effective method of decorating ice creams, mousses, and meringues.

Chocolate crumb crust

PREPARATION TIME 10 minutes   COOKING TIME 10 minutes   MAKES 1 x 9in. crumb crust

9oz. graham crackers
2 tbsp. unsweetened cocoa
    powder
6 tbsp. butter, melted

1   Preheat the oven to 400°F.

2   Break up the crackers roughly with your hands and then pulse them in a food processor (or place them in a plastic bag and crush with a rolling pin) until they are fine crumbs. Add the cocoa and melted butter and pulse until the mixture is well combined.

3   Empty the mixture into a greased 9in. springform pan, press it over the bottom and up the sides of the pan (according to the recipe), and bake in the hot oven 10 minutes. Remove from the oven and let the crust cool completely before removing it from the pan.

Creamy thick chocolate custard

PREPARATION TIME 10 minutes   COOKING TIME 10 minutes   MAKES 3¼ cups

1¾ cups milk
1¾ cups heavy cream
8 egg yolks
⅔ cup sugar
2 tbsp. unsweetened cocoa
    powder
1 tsp. vanilla extract

1   In a small saucepan, heat the milk and cream over low heat, until just warm. In a large bowl, whisk the egg yolks, sugar, and cocoa together, using a hand whisk, then whisk in the warm milk mixture. Return the mixture to the pan with the vanilla extract and stir constantly with a wooden spoon until the mixture begins to thicken and coats the back of the spoon. Do not boil.

2   Transfer to a clean bowl and let cool completely.

Fresh caramel sauce

PREPARATION TIME 5 minutes   COOKING TIME 5 minutes   MAKES 2 cups

½ cup plus 2 tsp. sugar
½ stick plus 1½ tsp. butter, chopped
1 cup plus 2 tbsp. heavy cream

1   In a medium-sized saucepan, stir together the sugar and butter over low heat until they melt, using a wooden spoon. Continue stirring gently until the mixture turns a light caramel color.

2   Remove the pan from the heat and add the cream (the sugar mixture will spatter, so be careful not to burn your hand), then return the pan to the heat and stir until well combined.

3   Pour the sauce into an airtight jar and set aside to cool completely before placing in the refrigerator. It will keep 2 to 3 days.

Choux pastry

PREPARATION TIME 10 minutes   COOKING TIME 5 minutes   MAKES 6 large éclairs or 12 profiteroles

2 tsp. sugar
5 tbsp. chilled butter, chopped
¾ cup all-purpose flour, sifted
2 eggs, lightly beaten

1   In a medium-sized saucepan, combine the sugar, butter, and ¾ cup water over low heat and stir constantly until the butter has just melted. Remove from the heat and add the flour all at once to the butter mixture, stirring well with a wooden spoon. (The mixture will form a thick dough.)

2   Return the saucepan to the heat and continue stirring 1 minute, or until the dough comes away from the sides of the saucepan.

3   Remove the saucepan from the heat and beat in the eggs, using an electric hand mixer. For best results, use the dough while still warm.

Sweet shortcrust pastry

PREPARATION TIME 10 minutes, plus chilling   COOKING TIME 30–35 minutes

MAKES 1 x 9in. pastry shell or 4 to 6 individual pastry shells

2 cups all-purpose flour, plus extra for rolling out

3 tbsp. powdered sugar

1 stick plus 3 tbsp. chilled butter, chopped

2 egg yolks

1   In a large bowl, combine the flour and powdered sugar. Add the butter and rub it in with your fingertips until it forms small crumbs. (Alternatively, do this in a food processor, but work quickly or the crust will be tough.) Work in the egg yolks and just enough of 2 tbsp. iced water to form a dough, using a flat-bladed knife or spatula. Note that the less water you use, the more tender the crust will be. Wrap the dough in plastic wrap and refrigerate 15 minutes.

2   Preheat the oven to 350°F. Roll out the dough on a lightly floured surface to about ¼in. thick, to fit a 9in. fluted loose-bottomed tart pan, 1½in. deep. Place the dough in the pan to form a pastry shell, taking care not to stretch it, and trim around the edge.

3   Line the pastry shell with baking paper and fill with baking beans. Bake in the hot oven 20 to 25 minutes, then remove from the oven and gently lift out the paper and beans. Return the pan to the oven a further 8 to 10 minutes, or until the pastry is dry and golden brown. (Alternatively, divide the pastry into 4 or 6 pieces and roll each one out to fit a 4in. fluted loose-bottomed tart pan, 1½in. deep, and bake 10 to 12 minutes, then a further 5 to 7 minutes.)

variation *To make Chocolate Shortcrust Pastry, add 1 tbsp. unsweetened cocoa powder with the flour and bake the dough until it is dry and dark brown.*

Quick-fix desserts

This chapter
offers a selection of
superb desserts that can be
made in a flash with the minimum
of fuss and effort. From White
Chocolate & Raspberry Eton Mess to
Chocolate Zabaglione, these simple
and easy recipes are a delight to
make and are just as impressive
as any time-consuming
creation.

Chocolate zabaglione

PREPARATION TIME 10 minutes   COOKING TIME 7–8 minutes

8 egg yolks
¼ cup sugar
5 tbsp. Marsala wine
3½oz. bittersweet chocolate,
    melted and left to cool
4 Italian ladyfinger cookies

1   In a large, heatproof bowl, beat together the yolks, sugar, and Marsala wine, using an electric hand mixer. Place the bowl over a pan of gently simmering water (making sure that the bowl does not touch the water or the eggs will scramble). Whisk vigorously until the mixture is frothy and just starting to thicken (this will take about 7 to 8 minutes), using a hand whisk.

2   Remove the bowl from the heat and beat in the melted chocolate, using an electric hand mixer.

3   Using a large spoon, divide the mixture evenly between 4 dishes. Serve immediately, accompanied by the ladyfingers.

Chocolate & chestnut mess

PREPARATION TIME 10 minutes

1¼ cups plus 1 tbsp. heavy cream
6 tbsp. canned, sweetened chestnut purée
4½oz. bittersweet chocolate, grated
2 tbsp. coffee liqueur
1 tbsp. sugar
8 crispy-style meringues

1 In a large bowl, whip the cream and chestnut purée until the mixture is just beginning to thicken, using an electric hand mixer. Add 3½oz. of the grated chocolate, the liqueur, and sugar and whip until the mixture is smooth and holds its shape lightly (taking care not to over-whip).

2 Put the meringues in a plastic bag, crush them lightly with a rolling pin, then empty them into the cream mixture and fold in, using a metal spoon.

3 Spoon the mixture into 4 dishes and sprinkle the remaining grated chocolate over the top.

White chocolate & raspberry Eton mess

PREPARATION TIME 10 minutes

1¼ cups heavy cream
1 tbsp. sugar
2 tbsp. raspberry liqueur
8 crispy-style meringues
3½oz. white chocolate, melted
and left to cool
1 cup raspberries, lightly
crushed

1 In a large bowl, whip the cream, sugar, and liqueur together until the mixture just forms soft peaks, using an electric hand mixer.

2 Put the meringues in a plastic bag, crush them lightly with a rolling pin, then empty them into the cream mixture and mix together, using a wooden spoon. Fold in the melted chocolate and raspberries.

3 Spoon the mixture into 4 dishes and serve immediately.

Chocolate liqueur fondue

PREPARATION TIME 10 minutes   COOKING TIME 5 minutes

10½oz. bittersweet chocolate,
  broken into pieces
¾ cup plus 1 tbsp. heavy
  cream
1 tsp. instant coffee powder
1 tbsp. coffee or hazelnut
  liqueur
1 tsp. vanilla extract
ladyfinger cookies, for dipping

1 In a medium-sized saucepan, heat the chocolate, cream, and coffee together over low heat until the chocolate is just melted. Remove the pan from the heat and stir the mixture with a wooden spoon until smooth. Stir in the liqueur and the vanilla extract.

2 Pour the fondue into a fondue bowl or small dish and serve immediately with the ladyfingers for dipping.

Quick tiramisu with chocolate

PREPARATION TIME 10 minutes

7oz. mascarpone cheese, softened

2 egg yolks

¾ cup plus 1 tbsp. powdered sugar, sifted

¾ cup plus 2 tbsp. heavy cream

3½oz. bittersweet or semi-sweet chocolate, melted and left to cool

6 ladyfinger cookies

½ cup strong coffee

¼ cup Marsala wine

¼ cup chocolate shavings

1 In a large bowl, beat the mascarpone, egg yolks, and powdered sugar together, using an electric hand mixer. Blend in the cream and melted chocolate.

2 Break the ladyfingers up into small pieces and divide them evenly between 4 dishes.

3 In a small bowl, combine the coffee and Marsala wine and pour this over the ladyfingers, then spoon the mascarpone mixture over the cookies. Top with the chocolate shavings before serving.

Quickest-ever dark chocolate mousse

PREPARATION TIME 10 minutes, plus chilling

2 egg whites
5 tbsp. sugar
7oz. bittersweet chocolate, melted and left to cool
1 cup plus 2 tbsp. heavy cream, whipped to soft peaks

1 In a large bowl, whisk the egg whites until soft peaks form, using an electric hand mixer. Add the sugar gradually while continuing to whisk until the whites are thick and shiny. Using a metal spoon, fold in the melted chocolate and cream.

2 Using a large spoon, divide the mousse between 4 dishes and refrigerate 30 minutes before serving.

Strawberries Romanoff with white chocolate

PREPARATION TIME 40 minutes, plus chilling

2 cups strawberries, hulled
    and sliced
2 tbsp. orange liqueur
2 tbsp. powdered sugar
1 cup plus 2 tbsp. heavy
    cream
1 tbsp. sugar
3½oz. white chocolate, melted
    and cooled

1   In a large bowl, stir together the strawberries, liqueur, and powdered sugar. Refrigerate the mixture 30 minutes to allow the flavors to mingle.

2   In a clean bowl, whisk the heavy cream and sugar together to form soft peaks, using an electric hand mixer, then stir in the melted chocolate. Purée half of the strawberry mixture in a blender, then, using a metal spoon, gently fold it into the cream mixture with the remaining strawberries.

3   Divide the mixture evenly between 4 dishes.

Roast figs with chocolate sauce

PREPARATION TIME 10 minutes   COOKING TIME 15–20 minutes

6 tbsp. butter, plus extra
  for greasing
8 large figs
2 tbsp. sugar
1 cup plus 2 tbsp. heavy
  cream, whipped to soft
  peaks
1 recipe quantity Rich
  Chocolate Sauce
  (see page 188)

1   Preheat the oven to 350°F. Grease a baking dish
(large enough to hold the figs) with butter.

2   Cut a cross in the top of each fig, taking care to keep
the fig in one piece. Divide the butter into 8 pieces
and place one piece inside each fig. Place the figs in the
prepared dish and sprinkle with the sugar.

3   Bake in the hot oven 15 to 20 minutes, or until
the figs are soft but still hold their shape. Remove from
the oven and set the baked figs aside in the dish to
cool 10 minutes.

4   Divide the figs between 4 plates and top with a
spoonful of cream and the rich chocolate sauce.

Chocolate heaven desserts

While chocolate cakes, bakes and desserts are, by their very nature, heavenly, sometimes the occasion calls for something just a little extra-special. The recipes in this chapter take chocolate that one step further—they are perfect for a special celebration or for when you just feel like being a bit more indulgent...

Mocha marble cheesecake

PREPARATION TIME 25 minutes, plus chilling   COOKING TIME 40–45 minutes

MAKES 1 x 9in. cheesecake

butter, for greasing

1 recipe quantity Chocolate Crumb Crust (see page 13)

10½oz. cream cheese, softened

7oz. ricotta cheese

¾ cup plus 2 tbsp. sugar

3 tsp. cornstarch

3 eggs, lightly beaten

2 tsp. vanilla extract

2 cups plus 1 tbsp. crème fraîche

1 cup plus 1 tbsp. heavy cream

2 tsp. instant coffee powder

2 tbsp. coffee liqueur

3½oz. bittersweet chocolate, melted and left to cool

1 Preheat the oven to 325°F. Grease a 9in. springform pan with butter and press the prepared chocolate crumb crust into the bottom.

2 In a large bowl, beat the cream cheese, ricotta, and sugar together, using an electric hand mixer, until smooth. Add the cornstarch, eggs, and vanilla extract and beat until just combined, then stir in the crème fraîche and cream. Divide the mixture evenly between 2 bowls. Blend the coffee, liqueur, and melted chocolate into one half of the mixture, using the electric hand mixer, and leave the other half plain.

3 Pour both of the mixtures over the crumb crust (use two hands and do this at the same time, if possible). Using a fork, swirl the mixtures together to create a marbled effect.

4 Bake in the hot oven 40 to 45 minutes, or until the cheesecake is firm around the edges but still slightly wobbly in the middle. Remove from the oven and let cool in the pan completely.

5 Refrigerate the cheesecake 2 hours or overnight, then remove from the pan.

Mini white chocolate cheesecakes

PREPARATION TIME 30 minutes, plus chilling   COOKING TIME 20–25 minutes

MAKES 6 mini cheesecakes

butter, for greasing
½ recipe quantity Chocolate
   Crumb Crust (see page 13)
7oz. cream cheese, softened
5 tbsp. sugar
1 egg, lightly beaten
4½oz. white chocolate, melted
   and left to cool
scant ½ cup heavy cream

1   Preheat the oven to 350°F. Grease 6 holes of a large muffin pan with butter and line each with a strip of baking paper, extending it up the sides. Divide the crumb crust mixture evenly between the holes and press down firmly to form the bottoms of the cheesecakes.

2   In a large bowl, beat the cream cheese and sugar together until light and fluffy, using an electric hand mixer, then beat in the egg. Stir in the melted chocolate and cream, using a wooden spoon, then divide the mixture between the holes.

3   Bake in the hot oven 20 to 25 minutes, or until the cheesecakes are just set and beginning to brown. Remove from the oven and let cool in the pan 15 minutes.

4   Remove the cheesecakes from the pan, using the strips of baking paper to help you, transfer to individual plates, and let cool completely. Chill 1 hour before serving.

Raspberry ripple white chocolate cheesecake

PREPARATION TIME 25 minutes, plus chilling   COOKING TIME 45–50 minutes

MAKES 1 x 9in. cheesecake

butter, for greasing
1 recipe quantity Chocolate
   Crumb Crust (see page 13)
1lb. 2oz. cream cheese,
   softened
¾ cup plus 2 tbsp. sugar
2 tbsp. all-purpose flour
4 eggs, lightly beaten
9oz. white chocolate, melted
   and left to cool
2 tsp. vanilla extract
½ cup heavy cream
1 cup raspberries, puréed

1   Preheat the oven to 350°F. Grease a 9in. springform pan with butter and press the prepared chocolate crumb crust into the bottom.

2   In a large bowl, beat the cream cheese and sugar together until light and creamy, using an electric hand mixer. Add the flour, eggs, melted chocolate, and vanilla extract and beat until just combined. Stir in the cream. Gently swirl through the raspberry purée, using a wooden spoon and taking care not to over-mix. Pour the filling mixture over the crumb crust.

3   Bake in the hot oven 45 to 50 minutes, or until the cheesecake is firm around the edges but still slightly wobbly in the middle. Remove from the oven and let cool in the pan completely.

4   Refrigerate the cheesecake 2 hours or overnight, then remove from the pan.

White chocolate & lime tart

PREPARATION TIME 15 minutes, plus chilling   COOKING TIME 5 minutes

MAKES 1 x 9in. tart

¾ cup plus 1 tbsp. heavy cream

10½oz. white chocolate, broken into pieces

zest of 2 limes, plus 1 lime, thinly sliced

1 Chocolate Crumb Crust, baked (see page 13)

1   In a small saucepan, heat the cream and chocolate together over low heat until the chocolate is just melted, then remove from the heat and stir until smooth, using a wooden spoon. Stir in the lime zest, then set aside to cool 10 minutes.

2   Pour the mixture into the baked crumb crust and refrigerate 2 hours or until set. Decorate with lime slices before serving.

Profiteroles with coffee cream & chocolate sauce

PREPARATION TIME 40 minutes   COOKING TIME 20–25 minutes

MAKES 12 profiteroles

1 recipe quantity Choux Pastry (see page 14)
1 cup plus 2 tbsp. heavy cream
2 tsp. instant coffee powder
1 tbsp. coffee liqueur
2 tbsp. sugar
1 recipe quantity Rich Chocolate Sauce (see page 188)

1 Preheat the oven to 425°F. Line a large baking sheet with baking paper. Spoon 12 tablespoonfuls of the choux pastry onto the baking sheet and sprinkle lightly with water.

2 Bake in the hot oven 20 to 25 minutes, or until the profiteroles are a deep golden brown. It is important to make sure that the middles are as dry as possible to achieve the best result.

3 Remove the profiteroles from the oven and transfer to a wire rack. Pierce each profiterole with a small, sharp knife to make a tiny hole through which the steam can escape. Let cool completely, then split horizontally and scrape out any wet dough that remains.

4 For the filling, put the cream, coffee, liqueur, and sugar in a bowl and whip to soft peaks, using an electric hand mixer. Spoon the creamy filling into the profiteroles. Place 3 profiteroles on each plate and pour the rich chocolate sauce over.

Strawberry & chocolate mille-feuilles

PREPARATION TIME 45 minutes, plus cooling   COOKING TIME 15–20 minutes

13oz. ready-rolled puff pastry
2 tbsp. milk
4 tsp. sugar
1 cup plus 2 tbsp. heavy
   cream, whipped to soft
   peaks
1 cup strawberries, hulled
   and thinly sliced
3½oz. bittersweet or milk
   chocolate, melted and
   left to cool
powdered sugar, sifted,
   for dusting

1   Preheat the oven to 375°F. Roll the pastry out on a lightly floured surface to ½in. thick. Cut into 8 rectangles, each about 4 x 2¾in. Place the rectangles on a large baking sheet and lightly brush the top of each one with milk. Using a fork, prick the pastry in 5 or 6 places, then sprinkle with sugar.

2   Bake the rectangles in the hot oven 15 to 20 minutes, or until the pastry rises and is golden brown. Remove from the oven and let the rectangles cool completely on the baking sheet.

3   To assemble the mille-feuilles, place a rectangle on each plate and spread a spoonful of whipped cream over. Top the cream with one-eighth of the strawberries and drizzle over one-eighth of the melted chocolate. Repeat with a second set of layers—pastry, cream, strawberries, and chocolate—then dust the mille-feuilles with powdered sugar and serve immediately.

Chocolate nut bavarois

PREPARATION TIME 25 minutes, plus cooling and chilling   COOKING TIME 5 minutes

¾ cup plus 1 tbsp. milk
2 tbsp. chocolate hazelnut
  paste
2 tbsp. hazelnut liqueur
3½oz. bittersweet or milk
  chocolate, broken into
  pieces
3 sheets leaf gelatin
4 egg yolks
3 tbsp. plus 1 tsp. sugar
1 cup plus 2 tbsp. heavy
  cream, whipped to
  soft peaks
chocolate curls, to sprinkle
  (optional)

1 In a medium-sized saucepan, heat the milk, chocolate hazelnut paste, liqueur, and chocolate over low heat until the chocolate has melted, stirring constantly with a wooden spoon. Remove from the heat and stir until smooth, then set aside to cool.

2 Meanwhile, soak the gelatin sheets in a bowl of cold water 5 to 10 minutes until soft, then remove them, wring out any excess water, and stir into the chocolate mixture until they dissolve. In a clean bowl, beat the egg yolks and sugar together, using a hand whisk, then gradually add to the cooled chocolate mixture. Pour into a clean bowl and set aside about 1½ hours until cool and beginning to thicken.

3 Gently fold in the cream, using a metal spoon, then pour the mixture into a 2-cup gelatin mold. Refrigerate 3 hours or overnight. Sprinkle with chocolate curls, if desired, before serving.

White chocolate panna cottas

PREPARATION TIME 15 minutes, plus cooling and chilling   COOKING TIME 5 minutes

3 sheets leaf gelatin
1 cup plus 2 tbsp. heavy
    cream
½ cup milk
3½oz. white chocolate, broken
    into pieces
2 tbsp. sugar
1 tsp. vanilla extract
1 cup raspberries
2 tbsp. powdered sugar, sifted

1 Soak the gelatin sheets in a bowl of cold water 5 to 10 minutes until soft.

2 In a small saucepan, heat the cream, milk, chocolate, sugar, and vanilla extract together over low heat until the chocolate is just melted. Remove from the heat and stir with a wooden spoon until smooth. Remove the gelatin from the water and wring out any excess. Drop the gelatin into the cream mixture and stir briefly until dissolved.

3 Divide the mixture evenly between 4 x ½-cup molds on a tray and set aside to cool about 30 minutes. Refrigerate the panna cottas 3 hours or overnight.

4 In a blender, pulse the raspberries to a purée with the powdered sugar to make a coulis. Dip the molds briefly into hot water and run a sharp knife around the sides. Turn the panna cottas out onto 4 plates and serve with the coulis.

White chocolate mousse with raspberries

PREPARATION TIME 20 minutes, plus chilling   COOKING TIME 5 minutes

1½ cups raspberries, plus
    extra for serving (optional)
⅔ cup milk
7oz. white chocolate, broken
    into pieces
1 tsp. vanilla extract
2 sheets leaf gelatin
¾ cup plus 1 tbsp. heavy
    cream, whipped to soft
    peaks
chocolate curls, for decorating

1   Divide the raspberries evenly between 4 small glasses.
In a small saucepan, heat the milk, white chocolate, and
vanilla extract over low heat until the chocolate is just
melted, stirring frequently with a wooden spoon.

2   In a small bowl, soak the gelatin in cold water until
soft. Remove the gelatin from the bowl and squeeze out
any excess water, then stir the gelatin into the chocolate
milk until dissolved. Pour into a clean bowl and set aside
until cool and beginning to thicken. Fold the whipped
cream into the chocolate mixture using a metal spoon,
then spoon the resulting mousse over the raspberries
in the glasses. Refrigerate 3 hours or overnight.

3   Use the chocolate curls and the extra raspberries,
if using, to decorate the top of each mousse.

Black cherry trifle

PREPARATION TIME 30 minutes, plus chilling   SERVES 4–6

7oz. ladyfinger cookies or
  plain sponge cake, sliced
¼ cup cherry brandy
2 cups canned cherries,
  drained, syrup reserved
1 recipe quantity Creamy
  Thick Chocolate Custard
  (see page 13)
1 cup plus 2 tbsp. heavy
  cream
2 tbsp. sugar
3½oz. bittersweet chocolate,
  melted and left to cool
6 ripe cherries

1   Place the ladyfingers or sliced cake into the bottom of
a large serving bowl and sprinkle with the cherry brandy.
Scatter the cherries over the ladyfingers or cake, along
with ¼ cup of the reserved syrup, then top with the
creamy thick chocolate custard.

2   In a large bowl, whip the cream with the sugar until
thick but not too stiff, using an electric hand mixer, then
spread it over the custard in the bowl. Drizzle over half
of the melted chocolate. Refrigerate the trifle 2 hours
or overnight.

3   Meanwhile, half-dip the cherries in the remaining
melted chocolate, let them set on the baking paper, and
then use to decorate the trifle.

Dark chocolate tiramisu

PREPARATION TIME 20 minutes, plus chilling   SERVES 4–6

2 eggs, separated, plus
  3 yolks
⅓ cup plus 4 tsp. sugar
9oz. mascarpone cheese,
  softened
3½oz. bittersweet chocolate,
  melted and left to cool,
  plus ¼ cup grated
1½ cups strong coffee
¼ cup Marsala wine
20 ladyfinger cookies
2 tbsp. unsweetened cocoa
  powder, sifted

1 In a large bowl, beat all the egg yolks and the sugar together until light and creamy, using an electric hand mixer. Blend in the mascarpone and melted chocolate until combined. In a clean bowl, whisk the egg whites until stiff but not dry, using clean attachments for the electric hand mixer, then, using a metal spoon, fold the whisked whites into the mascarpone mixture.

2 In a clean bowl, combine the coffee and Marsala wine and dip the ladyfingers into the mixture, allowing them to soak up some of the liquid.

3 Use 10 of the soaked ladyfingers to line the bottom of a serving dish about 11 x 7 x 2½in. Pour half the mascarpone mixture over the cookie layer, then cover with the remaining ladyfingers, followed by the remaining mascarpone. Dust the top with cocoa, sprinkle with the grated chocolate, and refrigerate 2 hours before serving.

Passionfruit, white chocolate & strawberry meringue roulade

PREPARATION TIME 25 minutes, plus cooling   COOKING TIME 15–18 minutes   SERVES 4–6

melted butter, for greasing
4 egg whites
pinch salt
1 cup plus 4 tsp. sugar
1 cup plus 2 tbsp. heavy
   cream, whipped to soft
   peaks
5½oz. white chocolate, melted
   and left to cool
2 cups strawberries, hulled
   and sliced
4 passionfruit
powdered sugar, sifted,
   for dusting

1   Preheat the oven to 325°F. Line a 9 x 13in. jelly roll pan with baking paper, so that the paper hangs over the edge. Lightly grease the paper with melted butter.

2   In a large bowl, whisk the egg whites with the salt until soft peaks form, using an electric hand mixer, then gradually add the sugar and continue whisking until stiff. Spread the meringue mixture over the prepared pan, using a palette knife.

3   Bake in the hot oven 15 to 18 minutes, or until the surface is crisp. Remove from the oven and let cool completely in the pan.

4   Turn the roulade out onto a large piece of baking paper and peel off the lining paper. In a large bowl, fold the cream and melted chocolate together, using a metal spoon. Using a palette knife, spread the cream mixture evenly over the roulade, then cover with the strawberries. Remove the pulp from the passionfruit, using a sharp knife, and scatter it over the strawberries.

5   Using the paper to help you, but making sure that it does not get trapped inside the roulade, gradually roll up the meringue jelly-roll style from a short end. Transfer carefully to a serving plate and dust with powdered sugar before serving.

Chocolate meringues with blackberries

PREPARATION TIME 15 minutes, plus cooling   COOKING TIME 40 minutes

MAKES 8–10 meringues

3 egg whites

⅔ cup sugar

1¾oz. bittersweet chocolate, grated, plus 1¾oz. melted and left to cool

1 tsp. cocoa powder

1 recipe quantity Chocolate Chantilly Cream (see page 194)

1½ cups blackberries

powdered sugar, sifted, for dusting

1 Preheat the oven to 275°F. Line 2 baking sheets with baking paper.

2 In a bowl, whisk the egg whites until stiff peaks form, using an electric hand mixer, then gradually whisk in the sugar until the mixture is thick and shiny and the sugar dissolves. Gently fold in the grated chocolate and cocoa, using a metal spoon. Place 16 to 20 heaped tablespoonfuls of the meringue mixture on the prepared sheets.

3 Bake in the warm oven 40 minutes, then turn the oven off and let the meringues cool completely in the oven.

4 Remove the meringues from the oven and sandwich them together in pairs with the chocolate Chantilly cream. Divide between 4 plates and drizzle with the melted chocolate. Serve with the blackberries, dusted with powdered sugar.

Irish coffee meringue with chocolate

PREPARATION TIME 30 minutes, plus cooling   COOKING TIME 60 minutes

MAKES 1 x 9in. meringue

6 egg whites
1⅓ cups sugar
1 tbsp. instant coffee powder
1 tbsp. unsweetened cocoa
  powder
1½ cups plus 2 tbsp. heavy
  cream
2 tbsp. coffee liqueur
3½oz. bittersweet chocolate,
  melted and cooled

1 Preheat the oven to 200°F. Line 2 baking sheets with baking paper and draw 2 x 9in. circles on the paper in pencil.

2 In a bowl, whisk the egg whites until stiff peaks form, using an electric hand mixer, then gradually whisk in the sugar until the mixture is thick and shiny and the sugar dissolves. Whisk in the coffee and cocoa. Spoon the mixture onto the prepared sheets and, using a palette knife, spread it over the circles on the baking paper.

3 Bake in the warm oven 60 minutes until the meringue is crisp but not brown. Remove from the oven and let the meringues cool completely on the sheets.

4 In a clean bowl, whisk the cream and liqueur together, using an electric hand mixer, to form soft peaks. To assemble the meringue, place 1 round on a serving tray, spread with half the liqueur cream and drizzle with half the melted chocolate. Repeat with the second meringue, remaining cream, and chocolate for the top layer, then refrigerate the meringue 2 hours before serving.

Chilled chocolate & raspberry soufflés

PREPARATION TIME 30 minutes, plus chilling   COOKING TIME 5 minutes

1 cup plus 2 tbsp. milk
2¾oz. bittersweet chocolate,
    broken into pieces
3 egg yolks
¼ cup sugar
3 sheets leaf gelatin
½ cup puréed raspberries
¾ cup plus 1 tbsp. heavy
    cream, whipped to
    soft peaks

1   Prepare 4 x 5oz. soufflé dishes by wrapping a 2in. wide strip of foil around the outside of each dish and tying it in place with string. The foil should stand ¾in. above the rim of the dish.

2   In a small saucepan, heat the milk and chocolate together over low heat until just melted, then remove the pan from the heat and stir with a wooden spoon until smooth. In a large bowl, whisk the yolks and sugar together, using an electric hand mixer, then whisk in the warm chocolate milk. Return the pan to the heat and continue cooking, stirring constantly with a wooden spoon, until the mixture thickens and coats the back of the spoon. Do not allow to boil.

3   Meanwhile, in a bowl, soak the gelatin sheets in cold water 5 to 10 minutes until soft, then remove them, wring out any excess water, and stir into the warm custard until they dissolve. Pour the mixture into a clean bowl and let cool.

4   Gently fold the raspberry purée and cream into the cooled custard, using a metal spoon, then divide equally between the prepared dishes. Refrigerate 2 hours or overnight. Remove the foil collars before serving.

Hot chocolate soufflés

PREPARATION TIME 25 minutes   COOKING TIME 20–23 minutes

melted butter, for greasing
⅓ cup sugar, plus extra
    for coating
2 tbsp. cornstarch
1 cup plus 2 tbsp. milk
3½oz. bittersweet chocolate,
    broken into pieces
3 eggs, separated, plus
    2 whites
powdered sugar, sifted,
    for dusting

1 Preheat the oven to 375°F. Grease 4 x 6oz. ramekins or ovenproof cups with melted butter and coat lightly with sugar.

2 In a small bowl, mix the cornstarch to a paste with 2 tbsp. of the milk. In a medium-sized saucepan, heat the remaining milk with the chocolate and 3 tbsp. plus 1 tsp. of the sugar over low heat. When the chocolate has melted, whisk in the cornstarch paste, using a hand whisk. Continue whisking until the mixture boils and thickens, then turn down to a simmer and cook 1 minute more. Remove from the heat and allow to cool a few minutes before beating in the egg yolks. Set the mixture aside to cool completely.

3 In a large bowl, whisk all the egg whites to soft peaks, using an electric hand mixer, then add the remaining sugar and continue to whisk until stiff but not dry. Gently fold the whisked whites into the chocolate mixture, using a metal spoon, and divide equally between the prepared cups.

4 Bake in the hot oven 15 to 18 minutes, or until the soufflés rise well. Remove from the oven, dust with powdered sugar, and serve immediately.

Chocolate roulade with mixed berries & white chocolate cream

PREPARATION TIME 25 minutes   COOKING TIME 18–20 minutes   SERVES 4–6

butter, for greasing
¾ cup plus 1 tbsp. sugar
6 eggs, separated
6oz. bittersweet chocolate, melted and left to cool
2 tbsp. unsweetened cocoa powder
1 cup plus 2 tbsp. heavy cream, whipped to soft peaks
3½oz. white chocolate, melted and left to cool
1½ cups mixed berries
powdered sugar, sifted, for dusting

1   Preheat the oven to 350°F. Grease a 9 x 13in. jelly roll pan with butter and line the bottom and sides with baking paper.

2   In a large bowl, beat the sugar and egg yolks together, using an electric hand mixer, until thick and creamy. Stir in the melted bittersweet chocolate and cocoa, using a wooden spoon. In a clean bowl, whisk the egg whites until stiff but not dry, using clean attachments for the electric hand mixer, then gently fold into the chocolate mixture, using a metal spoon. Pour the mixture into the prepared pan and spread evenly, using a palette knife.

3   Bake in the hot oven 18 to 20 minutes, or until firm. Remove from the oven and let cool completely in the pan. When cool, turn out onto a clean dish towel and remove the lining paper.

4   In a large bowl, fold the cream and the melted white chocolate together, using a metal spoon, and spread evenly over the roulade. Scatter over the mixed berries, slicing any strawberries.

5   Using the dish towel to help you, but making sure that it does not get trapped inside the roulade, gradually roll up the roulade jelly-roll style from a short end. Transfer carefully to a serving plate, and dust with powdered sugar before serving.

Sticky chocolate cake

PREPARATION TIME 25 minutes   COOKING TIME 50–55 minutes

MAKES 1 x 9in. cake

2 sticks plus 2 tbsp. butter, plus extra for greasing

1 cup plus 2 tbsp. heavy cream

6oz. bittersweet chocolate, broken into pieces

1 tsp. instant coffee powder

1⅓ cups packed light brown sugar

4 eggs, lightly beaten

2 tsp. vanilla extract

1½ cups plus 2 tbsp. self-rising flour

1 tsp. ground cinnamon

1 tsp. ground nutmeg

1 cup raisins

¾ cup plus 2 tbsp. walnuts, chopped

1 recipe quantity Rich Chocolate Sauce (see page 188)

1   Preheat the oven to 325°F. Grease a 9in. springform pan with butter and line the bottom with baking paper.

2   In a small saucepan, heat the cream, chocolate, and coffee over low heat until the chocolate is just melted. Remove the pan from the heat and stir the mixture with a wooden spoon until smooth, then let cool. In a large bowl, beat the butter and sugar together, using an electric hand mixer, until light and creamy, then beat in the eggs gradually. Stir in the vanilla extract and chocolate mixture, using a wooden spoon. Gently fold in the flour, cinnamon, nutmeg, raisins, and walnuts, using a metal spoon, then pour the mixture into the prepared pan.

3   Bake in the hot oven 45 to 50 minutes, or until a skewer inserted into the middle comes out with just a few moist crumbs on it. Remove from the oven and let the cake cool in the pan 10 minutes.

4   Remove the cake from the pan and serve warm with the rich chocolate sauce.

150

Cakes & bakes

There is nothing more wonderful than the aroma of freshly baked cakes and cookies. Baking really is a very simple skill to master and requires only a light touch and good-quality, fresh ingredients. Here you will find a fantastic selection of recipes, for cakes, brownies, cookies, squares, scones and muffins.

Warm chocolate & nut torte

PREPARATION TIME 20 minutes   COOKING TIME 40–45 minutes

MAKES 1 x 9in. torte

1 stick plus 5 tbsp. butter, softened, plus extra for greasing
¾ cup plus 1 tbsp. superfine sugar
1 tsp. vanilla extract
3 eggs, lightly beaten
1¾ cups ground almonds
¾ cup walnuts, roasted and finely chopped
¼ cup all-purpose flour
½ tsp. baking powder
¼ cup Marsala wine
1 recipe quantity Dark Chocolate Ganache (see page 196)

1   Preheat the oven to 325°F. Grease a 9in. springform pan with butter and line the bottom with baking paper.

2   In a large bowl, beat the butter, sugar, and vanilla extract together until light and creamy, using an electric hand mixer. Beat in the eggs, one at a time. In a clean bowl, mix together the nuts, flour, and baking powder, using a wooden spoon. Fold into the butter mixture with the Marsala, then pour into the prepared pan.

3   Bake in the hot oven 40 to 45 minutes, or until the torte is lightly browned and firm in the middle. Remove from the oven and let the torte cool in the pan 10 minutes. Turn the torte out onto a wire rack and let cool completely.

4   To ice the torte, use a palette knife to spread the dark chocolate ganache over the top.

Flourless chocolate & citrus cake

PREPARATION TIME 25 minutes   COOKING TIME 45–50 minutes

MAKES 1 x 9in. cake

1½ sticks butter, melted and
    left to cool, plus extra for
    greasing
6 eggs, separated
¾ cup plus 2 tbsp. superfine
    sugar
zest of 1 orange, finely grated
zest of 1 lemon, finely grated
½ cup orange juice
1¼ cups ground almonds
2 tbsp. unsweetened cocoa
    powder
9oz. bittersweet chocolate,
    melted and left to cool
powdered sugar, sifted,
    for dusting

1   Preheat the oven to 350°F. Grease a deep 9in.
springform round cake pan with butter and line the
bottom with baking paper.

2   In a large bowl, beat the egg yolks, sugar, and orange
and lemon zest together until thick and pale, using
an electric hand mixer. Stir in the melted butter and
the orange juice. In a clean bowl, combine the ground
almonds and cocoa, then fold into the egg mixture. In a
clean bowl, whisk the egg whites to soft peaks, using clean
attachments for the electric hand mixer, then pour in the
melted chocolate and stir together. Fold into the cake
mixture until just combined, using a metal spoon, then
pour into the prepared pan.

3   Bake in the hot oven 45 to 50 minutes, or until the
cake is firm around the edges but still slightly soft in the
middle. Remove from the oven and let the cake cool
completely in the pan, then remove the cake from the pan
and dust with powdered sugar.

Easy fudge cake

PREPARATION TIME 15 minutes   COOKING TIME 25–30 minutes

MAKES 1 x 9in. cake

6 tbsp. butter, melted, plus extra for greasing

200g/7oz/1 cup plus 1 tbsp. packed light brown sugar

2 eggs, lightly beaten

1 tsp. vanilla extract

140g/5oz/1¼ cups self-rising flour

2 tbsp. unsweetened cocoa powder

1 recipe quantity Creamy Chocolate Icing (see page 202)

1   Preheat the oven to 350°F. Grease a 9in. springform pan with butter and line the bottom with baking paper.

2   In a large bowl, beat the butter and sugar together, using an electric hand mixer, then add the eggs and vanilla extract, beating until well combined. In another bowl, combine the flour and cocoa, then add to the sugar mixture with ½ cup hot water, stirring with a wooden spoon just until everything is moist. Pour into the prepared pan.

3   Bake in the hot oven 25 to 30 minutes, or until a skewer inserted into the middle of the cake comes out clean. Remove from the oven and let the cake cool in the pan 10 minutes, then turn out onto a wire rack to cool completely.

4   To ice the cake, use a palette knife to spread over the creamy chocolate icing.

Chocolate ricotta cake

PREPARATION TIME 20 minutes   COOKING TIME 30–35 minutes

MAKES 1 x 9in. cake

1 stick plus 3 tbsp. butter,
   softened, plus extra for
   greasing
⅓ cup plus 4 tsp. superfine
   sugar
5½oz. bittersweet chocolate,
   melted and left to cool
3 eggs, separated
9oz. ricotta cheese
1 cup ground almonds
2 tbsp. all-purpose flour
powdered sugar, sifted,
   for dusting

1   Preheat the oven to 325°F. Grease a 9in. springform pan with butter and line the bottom with baking paper.

2   In a large bowl, beat the butter and sugar together until light and fluffy, using an electric hand mixer. Add the melted chocolate, egg yolks, and ricotta, stirring with a wooden spoon until just combined, then stir in the ground almonds and flour. In a clean bowl, whisk the egg whites to soft peaks, using clean attachments for the electric hand mixer, then fold into the chocolate mixture. Pour into the prepared pan.

3   Bake in the hot oven 30 to 35 minutes until the cake is just firm around the edges but still wobbly in the middle. Remove from the oven and let cool in the pan 10 to 15 minutes, then remove the cake from the pan and transfer to a serving plate. Dust with powdered sugar and serve warm.

Chocolate angel food cake

PREPARATION TIME 15 minutes   COOKING TIME 45–50 minutes

MAKES 1 x 8½ x 4in. cake

6 eggs, separated
1 cup plus 2 tbsp. vegetable
   oil
1¼ cups chocolate drink mix
2¼ cups self-rising flour
1¾ cups superfine sugar
powdered sugar, sifted,
   for dusting

1   Preheat the oven to 300°F. Place an ungreased, loose-bottomed angel food cake pan on a baking sheet. (If you do not have an angel food cake pan, use a ring pan of the same diameter, but make only half of the recipe.)

2   Place the egg yolks, oil, chocolate drink mix, flour, sugar, and 1 cup plus 2 tbsp. water in a large bowl and mix on low speed with an electric hand mixer until just combined. Then beat at the highest setting 10 minutes. In a clean bowl, whisk the egg whites until stiff, using clean attachments for the electric hand mixer, then fold gently into the chocolate mixture using a metal spoon. Pour into the prepared pan.

3   Bake in the warm oven 45 to 50 minutes, or until the cake is firm when touched. Remove from the oven and turn the cake pan upside down on to a wire rack, then let the cake cool completely in the pan.

4   When cold, loosen the cake from the pan with a sharp knife, turn out onto a serving plate and dust with powdered sugar.

Chocolate pear upside-down cake

PREPARATION TIME 20 minutes   COOKING TIME 30–35 minutes

MAKES 1 x 9In. cake

1 stick plus 6 tbsp. butter, softened, plus extra for greasing

7oz. bittersweet chocolate, broken into pieces

⅔ cup plus 1½ tsp. superfine sugar

3 eggs, lightly beaten

1 tsp. vanilla extract

¾ cup plus 4 tsp. self-rising flour

3 tbsp. packed light brown sugar

3 pears, ripe but firm, peeled, cored, and sliced into quarters

1 Preheat the oven to 350°F. Grease a 9in. springform pan with butter and line the bottom with baking paper.

2 In a small saucepan, combine the butter, chocolate, and sugar over low heat until just melted, stirring with a wooden spoon. Remove from the heat and set aside to cool completely. Stir in the eggs, vanilla extract, and flour until just combined. Sprinkle the brown sugar over the bottom of the pan, arrange the pear quarters over the top in a spiral shape, and pour the chocolate batter over.

3 Bake in the hot oven 25 to 30 minutes, or until a skewer inserted in the middle of the cake comes out with just a few moist crumbs on it. Remove from the oven and let the cake cool in the pan 15 minutes, then turn out onto a wire rack to cool completely, pear side up.

White chocolate Sauternes cake

PREPARATION TIME 20 minutes   COOKING TIME 30–35 minutes

MAKES 1 x 9in. cake

1½ sticks butter, softened, plus extra for greasing

¾ cup plus 2 tbsp. superfine sugar

3 eggs, lightly beaten

1 cup all-purpose flour

¾ cup plus 4 tsp. self-rising flour

½ cup milk

⅓ cup Sauternes

7oz. white chocolate, melted and left to cool

1 recipe quantity White Chocolate Frosting (see page 201)

1 Preheat the oven to 350°F. Grease a 9in. springform pan with butter and line the bottom with baking paper.

2 In a large bowl, beat the butter and sugar together until light and creamy, using an electric hand mixer, then gradually beat in the eggs until smooth. In a clean bowl, combine the flours using a wooden spoon, then fold into the butter mixture with the milk and half of the Sauternes, using a metal spoon. Stir in the melted chocolate and pour the mixture into the prepared pan.

3 Bake in the hot oven 30 to 35 minutes, or until a skewer inserted into the middle of the cake comes out clean. Remove from the oven and let the cake cool in the pan 10 minutes, then turn out onto a wire rack to cool completely. Pierce a few holes in the top of the cake with a skewer, then drizzle with the remaining Sauternes. Let the cake cool completely.

4 To ice the cake, use a palette knife to spread the white chocolate frosting over the cake.

Chocolate cream roll with strawberries

PREPARATION TIME 35 minutes COOKING TIME 10–12 minutes

MAKES 1 x cream roll

butter, for greasing

4 eggs, separated

¾ cup plus 2 tbsp. superfine sugar, plus 2 tbsp. for sprinkling

2¾oz. bittersweet or milk chocolate, grated

½ cup plus 2 tbsp. self-rising flour

1 recipe quantity Chocolate Chantilly Cream (see page 194)

1 cup strawberries, hulled and sliced

1 Preheat the oven to 350°F. Grease a 9 x 13in. jelly roll pan with butter and line the bottom and sides with baking paper.

2 In a large bowl, beat the egg yolks and half the sugar together until thick and creamy, using an electric hand mixer. Stir in 2 tbsp. water, the grated chocolate, and flour, using a wooden spoon. In a clean bowl, whisk the egg whites to soft peaks, using clean attachments for the electric hand mixer, then continue whisking, gradually adding the remaining sugar, until thick and shiny. Fold into the chocolate mixture until just combined, using a metal spoon. Pour the mixture into the prepared pan and spread evenly, using a palette knife.

3 Bake in the hot oven 10 to 12 minutes, or until just firm. Remove from the oven and turn out onto a large sheet of baking paper that has been sprinkled with sugar. Remove the lining paper, then, using the baking paper to help you, roll up from a short side, enclosing the paper in the cake. Let cool completely.

4 When cool, unroll the cake carefully, spread with the chocolate Chantilly cream and scatter over the strawberries. Re-roll, transfer to a serving plate, and refrigerate until ready to serve.

Chocolate & almond marble cake

PREPARATION TIME 20 minutes   COOKING TIME 18–20 minutes

MAKES 1 x 9in. cake

1½ sticks butter, softened,
   plus extra for greasing
¾ cup superfine sugar
1 egg, lightly beaten
1 tsp. vanilla extract
1 cup ground almonds
¾ cup plus 4 tsp. self-rising
   flour
¼ cup milk
5½oz. milk chocolate, melted
   and left to cool
1 recipe quantity Dark
   Chocolate Ganache
   (see page 196)

1   Preheat the oven to 350°F. Grease an 9in. square cake pan with butter and line the bottom with baking paper.

2   In a large bowl, beat the butter and sugar together until light and fluffy, using an electric hand mixer. Gradually beat in the egg and vanilla extract until well combined. In a clean bowl, mix together the almonds and flour, using a wooden spoon, then gently fold into the butter mixture with the milk, using a metal spoon. Place half of the cake mixture into the prepared pan. Fold the melted chocolate into the remaining mixture and pour into the pan. Gently draw a fork through the mix to create a swirled effect.

3   Bake in the hot oven 18 to 20 minutes, or until the cake is just firm. Remove from the oven and let the cake cool in the pan 10 minutes, then turn out onto a wire rack to cool completely.

4   To ice the cake, use a palette knife to spread the dark chocolate ganache over the cake.

Orange loaf cake with chocolate chips

PREPARATION TIME 20 minutes   COOKING TIME 40–45 minutes

MAKES 1 x 9 x 4½in. loaf cake

1½ sticks butter, softened, plus extra for greasing

¾ cup plus 1 tbsp. superfine sugar

2 eggs, lightly beaten

1⅓ cups plus 4 tsp. self-rising flour

3½oz. bittersweet or milk chocolate chips

zest of 1 orange, grated, plus juice

1 tbsp. milk

1 recipe quantity Chocolate Buttercream (see page 194)

1 Preheat the oven to 350°F. Grease a 9 x 4½in. loaf pan with butter and line the bottom with baking paper.

2 In a large bowl, beat the butter and sugar together until light and fluffy, using an electric hand mixer, then gradually beat in the eggs. Fold in the flour, chocolate chips, orange zest, and milk until just combined and pour into the prepared pan.

3 Bake in the hot oven 40 to 45 minutes, or until a skewer inserted into the center comes out with just a few moist crumbs on it. Remove from the oven.

4 Pierce the top of the cake in 3 or 4 places with the skewer and brush over the orange juice. Cool 10 minutes, then turn out onto a wire rack and top with the chocolate buttercream.

Chocolate banana bread

PREPARATION TIME 20 minutes   COOKING TIME 50–55 minutes

MAKES 1 x 9 x 4½in. loaf

1 stick plus 1 tbsp. butter, softened, plus extra for greasing and to serve
⅔ cup packed light brown sugar
2 eggs, lightly beaten
5½oz. bittersweet chocolate, melted and left to cool
3 ripe bananas, mashed
1 tsp. vanilla extract
1½ cups plus 2 tbsp. self-rising flour

1 Preheat the oven to 350°F. Grease a 9 x 4½in. loaf pan with butter and line the bottom with baking paper.
2 In a large bowl, beat the butter and sugar together until light and fluffy, using an electric hand mixer. Add the eggs, beating well, then stir in the melted chocolate, bananas, vanilla extract, and flour until just combined, using a wooden spoon. Spoon into the prepared pan.
3 Bake in the hot oven 50 to 55 minutes, or until a skewer inserted into the middle of the cake comes out with just a few crumbs clinging to it. Remove from the oven and let the cake cool in the pan 10 minutes, then turn out onto a wire rack to cool completely. Serve with butter for spreading.

Pear, pistachio & chocolate loaf cake

PREPARATION TIME 30 minutes   COOKING TIME 55–60 minutes

MAKES 1 x 9 x 4½in. loaf cake

1 stick plus 3 tbsp. butter, softened, plus extra for greasing

⅔ cup plus 1½ tsp. superfine sugar

3 eggs, lightly beaten

1 tsp. vanilla extract

7oz. bittersweet chocolate, finely chopped

1 pear, peeled, cored, and diced

⅓ cup pistachio nuts

1 cup plus 3 tbsp. self-rising flour

1   Preheat the oven to 350°F. Grease a 9 x 4½in. loaf pan with butter.

2   In a large bowl, beat the butter and sugar together until light and fluffy, using an electric hand mixer. Add the eggs one at a time, whisking well in between, then add the vanilla extract. Fold in the chocolate, pear, pistachio nuts, and flour until just combined, using a wooden spoon. Pour into the prepared pan.

3   Bake in the hot oven 55 to 60 minutes, or until a skewer inserted into the middle of the cake comes out clean. Remove from the oven and let the cake cool in the pan 10 minutes, then turn out onto a wire rack to cool completely.

Chocolate ginger cake

PREPARATION TIME 25 minutes   COOKING TIME 35–40 minutes

MAKES 1 x 9in. cake

1 stick plus 3 tbsp. butter, softened, plus extra for greasing

¾ cup plus 2 tsp. packed light brown sugar

2 eggs, lightly beaten

2 tbsp. chopped candied ginger

1 tbsp. honey

3½oz. bittersweet chocolate, melted and left to cool

1 cup plus 3 tbsp. self-rising flour

2 tsp. ground ginger

1 tbsp. dark rum

1 recipe quantity Chocolate Rum Frosting (see page 199)

1 Preheat the oven to 350°F. Grease a 9in. square cake pan with butter and line the bottom with baking paper.

2 In a large bowl, beat the butter and sugar together until light and fluffy, using an electric hand mixer, then add the eggs and beat until smooth. Stir in the chopped ginger, honey, and melted chocolate until just combined, using a wooden spoon. Sift the flour and ground ginger together and fold into the cake mixture with the rum, using a metal spoon. Spoon into the prepared pan.

3 Bake in the hot oven 35 to 40 minutes, or until the cake is just firm in the middle. Remove from the oven and let the cake cool in the pan 10 minutes, then turn out onto a wire rack to cool completely.

4 To ice the cake, use a palette knife to spread the chocolate rum frosting over the cake.

Chocolate madeleines

PREPARATION TIME 15 minutes   COOKING TIME 15–17 minutes

MAKES 12–14 madeleines

7 tbsp. butter, chopped, plus
   extra for greasing
2¾oz. bittersweet chocolate,
   broken into pieces
½ cup plus 2 tbsp. all-purpose
   flour
½ tsp. baking powder
pinch salt
2 eggs
⅓ cup plus 4 tsp. superfine
   sugar
powdered sugar, sifted,
   for dusting

1   Preheat the oven to 350°F. Grease a 12-hole madeleine pan with butter.

2   In a small saucepan, heat the butter and chocolate together over low heat until just melted, then set aside to cool. Sift the flour and baking powder into a bowl, and add the salt. In a large bowl, beat the eggs and sugar together until the mixture is light in color, using an electric hand mixer, then whisk in the chocolate mixture. Using a metal spoon, gently fold in the flour mix, then divide the mixture between the holes in the prepared pan, taking care not to overfill.

3   Bake in the hot oven 10 to 12 minutes until the cakes are firm to the touch. Remove from the oven and let the madeleines cool in the pan 10 minutes, then turn out onto a wire rack to cool completely and dust with powdered sugar.

Dark & white chocolate brownies

PREPARATION TIME 25 minutes   COOKING TIME 20–25 minutes

MAKES 12 brownies

1½ sticks butter, chopped, plus extra for greasing
2 tbsp. unsweetened cocoa powder
1¼ cups plus 1 tbsp. superfine sugar
2 eggs, lightly beaten
1 tsp. vanilla extract
1 cup plus 3 tbsp. all-purpose flour
2¼oz. white chocolate chips
2¼oz. bittersweet chocolate chips
⅔ cup walnuts, roughly chopped

1   Preheat the oven to 350°F. Grease a shallow 9in. square pan with butter and line the bottom with baking paper, leaving some hanging over the edges to make removing the brownies easier.

2   In a large saucepan, heat the butter with the cocoa and sugar over low heat until just melted, remove from the heat and set aside to cool. When cool, add the remaining ingredients and stir with a wooden spoon until just combined. Pour into the prepared pan.

3   Bake in the hot oven 15 to 20 minutes, or until the brownie is firm around the edges and still slightly soft in the middle. Remove from the oven and let cool in the pan completely, then cut into 12 squares.

Cappuccino brownies

PREPARATION TIME 20 minutes COOKING TIME 20–25 minutes

MAKES 12 brownies

1½ sticks butter, chopped, plus extra for greasing

2 tbsp. unsweetened cocoa powder

2 tsp. instant coffee powder

1 cup plus 4 tsp. superfine sugar

2 eggs, lightly beaten

1 tsp. vanilla extract

1 cup plus 3 tbsp. all-purpose flour

1 recipe quantity White Chocolate Frosting (see page 201)

1 tbsp. unsweetened cocoa powder, sifted

1   Preheat the oven to 350°F. Grease a shallow 9in. square pan with butter and line the bottom with baking paper, leaving some hanging over the edges to make removing the brownies easier.

2   In a small saucepan, heat the butter with the cocoa, coffee, and sugar over low heat until just melted, remove from the heat and set aside to cool. When cool, add the eggs, vanilla extract, and flour and stir with a wooden spoon until just combined. Pour into the prepared pan.

3   Bake in the hot oven 15 to 20 minutes, or until the brownie is firm around the edges and still slightly soft in the middle. Remove from the oven and let cool completely in the pan.

4   To ice the brownie, use a palette knife to spread the white chocolate frosting over the top. Sprinkle with the cocoa, then cut into 12 squares.

White chocolate, lime & coconut cupcakes

PREPARATION TIME 20 minutes   COOKING TIME 18–20 minutes

MAKES 12 cupcakes

1 cup plus 3 tbsp. self-rising flour
3 tbsp. plus 1 tsp. superfine sugar
½ stick butter, melted
1 egg, lightly beaten
scant ½ cup milk
1 tsp. vanilla extract
juice and zest of 1 lime
3½oz. white chocolate, broken into pieces
½ cup flaked coconut
1 recipe quantity White Chocolate Frosting (see page 201)

1 Preheat the oven to 350°F. Line a 12-hole muffin pan with 12 paper muffin liners.

2 In a large bowl, combine the flour and sugar and make a well in the middle. Mix together the butter, egg, milk, vanilla extract, and lime juice and zest, using a wooden spoon, and stir into the flour mixture until just combined. Stir in the white chocolate and coconut, then divide the mixture evenly between the muffin liners.

3 Bake in the hot oven 18 to 20 minutes, or until the cupcakes are firm to the touch. Remove from the oven and transfer to wire racks to cool completely.

4 To ice the cupcakes, use a palette knife to spread the white chocolate frosting over the cupcakes.

Chocolate cupcakes

PREPARATION TIME 20 minutes   COOKING TIME 12–15 minutes

MAKES 12 cupcakes

1 stick plus 1 tbsp. butter, softened
½ cup plus 1 tsp. superfine sugar
2 eggs, lightly beaten
1 cup self-rising flour
3 tbsp. unsweetened cocoa powder
2 tbsp. milk
½ tsp. vanilla extract
1 recipe quantity Creamy Chocolate Icing (see page 202)

1   Preheat the oven to 350°F. Line a 12-hole muffin pan with 12 paper muffin liners.

2   In a large bowl, beat the butter and sugar until light and creamy, using an electric hand mixer, then gradually whisk in the eggs until well blended. In a clean bowl, sift the flour and cocoa together, then fold into the butter mixture, using a metal spoon, along with the milk and vanilla extract. Divide the mixture evenly between the muffin liners.

3   Bake in the hot oven 12 to 15 minutes, or until the cupcakes are firm to the touch. Remove from the oven and transfer to wire racks to cool completely.

4   To ice the cupcakes, use a palette knife to spread the creamy chocolate icing over the cupcakes.

Blondies

PREPARATION TIME 20 minutes   COOKING TIME 25–30 minutes
MAKES 12 blondies

7 tbsp. butter, chopped, plus
   extra for greasing
4½oz. white chocolate, broken
   into pieces
¾ cup plus 2 tbsp. superfine
   sugar
3 eggs, lightly beaten
1 tsp. vanilla extract
¾ cup hazelnuts, skinned and
   chopped
3½oz. white chocolate chips
1⅓ cups plus 4 tsp.
   all-purpose flour

1 Preheat the oven to 350°F. Grease a shallow 9in. square pan with butter and line the bottom with baking paper.
2 In a small saucepan, heat the butter and chocolate together over low heat until the chocolate is just melted, then remove from the heat and stir gently until smooth. In a large bowl, combine the sugar and eggs, then stir in the chocolate mixture, vanilla extract, hazelnuts, chocolate chips, and flour, using a wooden spoon. Pour into the prepared pan.
3 Bake in the hot oven 20 to 25 minutes, or until the cake is firm around the edges but still moist in the middle. Remove from the oven and let the cake cool in the pan completely. Remove the cake from the pan and cut into 12 squares.

Chocolate almond squares

PREPARATION TIME 15 minutes   COOKING TIME 20–25 minutes

MAKES 16 squares

7 tbsp. butter, softened, plus extra for greasing

5 tbsp. superfine sugar

4 eggs, separated

3½oz. bittersweet chocolate, grated

¼ cup all-purpose flour

1 tbsp. brandy

1 recipe quantity Shiny Chocolate Icing (see page 202)

1   Preheat the oven to 350°F. Grease a shallow 9in. square pan with butter, then line the bottom with baking paper.

2   In a large bowl, mix together the butter, sugar, egg yolks, chocolate, ground almonds, flour, and brandy, using a wooden spoon. In a clean bowl, whisk the egg whites to soft peaks, using an electric hand mixer, then fold into the chocolate mixture, using a metal spoon. Pour into the prepared pan.

3   Bake in the hot oven 20 to 25 minutes, or until the cake is firm and lightly browned. Remove from the oven and let cool completely in the pan.

4   To ice, use a palette knife to spread the shiny chocolate icing over the cake, then cut into 16 squares.

White chocolate fruit & nut bars

PREPARATION TIME 20 minutes   COOKING TIME 35–40 minutes

MAKES 16 bars

butter, for greasing
1 cup slivered almonds
2 cups walnuts, chopped
1⅔ cups desiccated coconut
¾ cup dried apricots, chopped
1 cup plus 2 tbsp. raisins
2 tbsp. plus 1 tsp. rice flour
¼ cup ground almonds
½ cup apricot jam
½ cup honey
9oz. white chocolate, melted
  and left to cool

1   Preheat the oven to 325°F. Grease a shallow 8 x 12in. pan with butter and line with baking paper.

2   In a large bowl, mix the almonds, walnuts, coconut, apricots, raisins, flour, and ground almonds together. In a small saucepan, gently warm the jam and honey together over low heat until melted. Pour the jam and honey mixture into the fruit mixture, stir well to combine, then pour into the prepared pan.

3   Bake in the hot oven 30 to 35 minutes, or until the slice is lightly browned. Remove from the oven and let the cake cool completely in the pan before spreading the melted chocolate over the top. Allow to set before cutting into 16 bars.

Chocolate oat bars

PREPARATION TIME 20 minutes   COOKING TIME 15–20 minutes

MAKES 18 bars

3 sticks butter, chopped, plus extra for greasing
3 tbsp. light corn syrup
¾ cup plus 3 tbsp. packed light brown sugar
⅓ cup plus 4 tsp. superfine sugar
5 tbsp. unsweetened cocoa powder
3½ cups rolled oats

1 Preheat the oven to 300°F. Grease a shallow 9in. square cake pan with butter and line the bottom with baking paper.

2 In a small saucepan, melt the butter with the light corn syrup, over low heat. Remove from the heat and set aside. In a large bowl, mix together both sugars, cocoa, and rolled oats, using a wooden spoon, then pour the butter mixture into the bowl. Stir until well combined then press the mixture into the prepared pan.

3 Bake in the warm oven 15 to 20 minutes, or until just firm in the middle. Remove from the oven and let cool completely in the pan before cutting into 18 bars.

Cranberry & white chocolate scones

PREPARATION TIME 20 minutes   COOKING TIME 15–20 minutes

MAKES 6 large scones

6 tbsp. butter, chilled and chopped, plus extra for greasing and to serve
2 cups self-rising flour
3 tbsp. plus 1 tsp. superfine sugar
2¾oz. white chocolate chips
¾ cup plus 1 tbsp. dried cranberries
6 tbsp. milk, plus extra for brushing
1 egg, lightly beaten

1   Preheat the oven to 375°F. Grease a large baking sheet with butter.

2   Place the flour and sugar in a large bowl and, working lightly, rub in the butter with your fingertips until the mixture resembles breadcrumbs. Stir in the chocolate chips and cranberries, using a wooden spoon. In a small bowl, beat together the milk and egg. Add the milk mixture to the flour mixture until it forms a soft dough, using a rounded knife and a cutting motion.

3   Turn the dough out on to a lightly floured board and pat it out until it is about 1in. thick. Cut out 6 circles, using a round cookie cutter, and place on the prepared sheet. Brush the tops with a little extra milk, using a pastry brush.

4   Bake in the hot oven 15 to 20 minutes, or until the scones are golden brown. Remove from the oven and transfer to a wire rack to cool completely, then transfer to a serving plate and serve warm or cold with butter.

White chocolate & blueberry muffins

PREPARATION TIME 15 minutes   COOKING TIME 15–20 minutes

MAKES 12 muffins

1 stick plus 1 tbsp. butter, melted, plus extra for greasing
2 cups self-rising flour
⅓ cup plus 4 tsp. superfine sugar
4½oz. white chocolate, broken into pieces
1 egg, lightly beaten
½ cup milk
1 tsp. vanilla extract
1 cup blueberries

1 Preheat the oven to 375°F. Grease a 12-hole muffin pan with butter.

2 In a large bowl, mix all the ingredients together until just combined, using a wooden spoon. Divide the mixture evenly into the prepared pan.

3 Bake in the hot oven 15 to 20 minutes until the muffins rise and are golden brown. Remove from the oven and let the muffins cool in the pan 5 to 10 minutes, then remove from the pan and transfer to a wire rack to cool completely.

Double chocolate muffins

PREPARATION TIME 15 minutes   COOKING TIME 20–25 minutes

MAKES 12 muffins

1 stick plus 1 tbsp. butter, melted, plus extra for greasing
3 cups self-rising flour
3 tbsp. unsweetened cocoa powder
¾ cup plus 1 tbsp. superfine sugar
2 eggs, lightly beaten
4½oz. bittersweet or milk chocolate chips
1 cup plus 2 tbsp. milk

1 Preheat the oven to 375°F. Grease a 12-hole muffin pan with butter.

2 In a large bowl, mix together all the ingredients until just combined, using a wooden spoon. Divide the mixture evenly into the prepared pan.

3 Bake in the hot oven 20 to 25 minutes until the muffins rise and are golden brown. Remove from the oven and let cool in the pan 5 to 10 minutes, then remove from the pan and transfer to a wire rack to cool completely.

Chocolate cherry macaroons

PREPARATION TIME 10 minutes, plus chilling   COOKING TIME 18–20 minutes

MAKES 20 macaroons

butter, for greasing
1⅔ cups flaked coconut
¾ cup plus 2 tbsp. coconut cream
2 tbsp. unsweetened cocoa powder
¾ cup plus 4 tsp. powdered sugar
2 large egg whites
½ cup candied cherries, finely chopped

1   Preheat the oven to 325°F. Line 2 large baking sheets with baking paper.

2   In a large bowl, mix all of the ingredients until well combined, using a wooden spoon. Refrigerate the mixture 30 minutes. Place 20 heaped teaspoonfuls of the mixture on the prepared baking sheet, leaving about 2in. between them to allow for spreading.

3   Bake in the hot oven 18 to 20 minutes, or until the macaroons look just firm. (You may need to cook them in batches.) Remove the macaroons from the oven and let cool on the sheets 5 minutes before transferring to a wire rack to cool completely.

Chocolate melting moments

PREPARATION TIME 20 minutes   COOKING TIME 8–10 minutes

MAKES 20 cookies

1 stick plus 1 tbsp. butter,
   softened, plus extra for
   greasing
¼ cup powdered sugar, plus
   extra, sifted, for dusting
1 cup all-purpose flour
3 tbsp. unsweetened cocoa
   powder

1   Preheat the oven to 350°F. Grease 2 large baking sheets with butter.

2   In a large bowl, mix the butter and sugar together, using a wooden spoon, until light and fluffy. In a clean bowl, combine the flour and cocoa, then stir into the butter mixture until just combined (the mixture will be soft). Place a little flour on your hands and roll the mixture into 20 balls. Place 10 balls of dough on each baking sheet, leaving about 2in. between them to allow for spreading, and press the top of each cookie down with a lightly floured fork.

3   Bake in the hot oven 8 to 10 minutes, or until the cookies are firm. (You may need to cook them in batches.) Remove the melting moments from the oven and let cool on the sheets 5 minutes before transferring to a wire rack to cool completely. Dust with the extra sugar.

Orange chocolate-chip cookies

PREPARATION TIME 20 minutes   COOKING TIME 10–12 minutes

MAKES 24 cookies

1 stick plus 1 tbsp. butter, softened, plus extra for greasing
1 tsp. vanilla extract
⅓ cup plus 1 tbsp. packed light brown sugar
5 tbsp. superfine sugar
1 egg, lightly beaten
1½ cups all-purpose flour
1 tsp. cardamom
1 tsp. cinnamon
zest of 1 orange, grated
7oz. orange-flavored chocolate, broken into pieces

1 Preheat the oven to 350°F. Grease 2 large baking sheets with butter.

2 In a large bowl, beat together the butter, vanilla extract, and both sugars until light and creamy, using an electric hand mixer. Add the egg until well combined, then stir in the remaining ingredients. Place 24 tablespoonfuls of the mixture on the prepared baking sheets, leaving about 2in. between them to allow for spreading.

3 Bake in the hot oven 10 to 12 minutes, or until the cookies are dark brown. (You may need to cook them in batches.) Remove the cookies from the oven and transfer to wire racks to cool completely.

Chocolate & pistachio biscotti

PREPARATION TIME 35 minutes   COOKING TIME 50–65 minutes

MAKES about 20 biscotti

½ cup plus 1 tsp. superfine sugar

1 egg

1 cup all-purpose flour

2 tbsp. unsweetened cocoa powder

½ tsp. baking powder

¾ cup pistachio nuts, roughly chopped

1   Preheat the oven to 325°F. Line a large baking sheet with baking paper.

2   In a large bowl, beat the sugar and egg together until pale and thick, using an electric hand mixer. In a separate bowl, combine the remaining ingredients, using a metal spoon, and fold into the egg mixture to form a dough. Remove the dough from the bowl and gently knead it on a lightly floured surface about 30 seconds. Form a log about 7 x 2in. in size and place on the prepared baking sheet.

3   Bake in the hot oven 20 to 25 minutes, or until the dough is firm to the touch. Remove from the oven, turning the temperature down to 275°F, and let cool completely. When the dough is cold, cut it into about 20 slices about ¼in. thick, using a serrated knife.

4   Place the biscotti slices on a fresh baking sheet and bake them in the warm oven 30 to 40 minutes, turning once, until they are very dry. Remove the biscotti from the oven and let cool completely.

Truffle dough cookies

PREPARATION TIME 15 minutes, plus chilling   COOKING TIME 10–12 minutes

MAKES 20 cookies

⅓ cup plus 4 tsp. superfine sugar
½ cup plus 2 tbsp. self-rising flour
3 tbsp. unsweetened cocoa powder
pinch salt
2 tbsp. butter, chopped
1 egg, lightly beaten
1 tsp. vanilla extract
powdered sugar, sifted, for rolling and dusting

1   Line a large baking sheet with baking paper.

2   Place the sugar, flour, cocoa, salt, and butter in the bowl of a food processor, and pulse 30 seconds. Add the egg and vanilla extract and pulse 15 seconds more, or until the mixture forms a dough. Remove the dough from the processor and refrigerate 30 minutes. Preheat the oven to 350°F.

3   Roll the dough into 20 balls about the size of a walnut, then roll these balls in powdered sugar and place on the prepared sheet, leaving about 4in. between them to allow for spreading.

4   Bake in the hot oven 10 to 12 minutes until the cookies are just set. (You may need to cook them in batches.) Remove the cookies from the oven and transfer to a wire rack to cool completely. Dust with powdered sugar.

Hazelnut thumbprints

PREPARATION TIME 20 minutes   COOKING TIME 10–12 minutes

MAKES 24 cookies

1 stick plus 1 tbsp. butter, softened, plus extra for greasing

½ cup plus 1 tsp. superfine sugar

1 egg, lightly beaten

½ cup plus 2 tbsp. all-purpose flour

½ cup plus 2 tbsp. self-rising flour

2 tbsp. unsweetened cocoa powder

⅔ cup chocolate hazelnut spread

powdered sugar, sifted, for dusting

1 Preheat the oven to 350°F. Grease 2 large baking sheets with butter.

2 In a large bowl, beat the butter and sugar together until pale and creamy, using an electric hand mixer, then add the egg, beating well to combine. In a separate bowl, mix together both flours and the cocoa, using a wooden spoon, and stir into the butter mixture to form a dough.

3 Roll teaspoonfuls of the dough into 24 balls and place on the prepared sheets, leaving about 2in. between them to allow for spreading. Push the middle of each ball of dough down with your thumb to create an indentation, then place a teaspoonful of the chocolate hazelnut spread into each indented hole.

4 Bake in the hot oven 10 to 12 minutes, or until the cookies are firm. (You may need to cook them in batches.) Remove the thumbprints from the oven and let cool on the sheets 10 minutes before transferring to a wire rack to cool completely. Dust with powdered sugar.

150

Pastries & puddings

In this chapter
you will find a range
of hot and cold puddings
and tarts that make the perfect
ending for any occasion. There is
something for everyone, with recipes
such as Chocolate Crèmes Brûlées
and Chocolate Croissant Pudding
providing delicious variations
on traditional comfort-food
family favorites.

Chocolate pancakes

PREPARATION TIME 10 minutes   COOKING TIME 15 minutes

MAKES about 12 pancakes

2 cups self-rising flour

1 tbsp. unsweetened cocoa
powder

⅓ cup plus 4 tsp. sugar

1 cup plus 2 tbsp. milk

1 egg, lightly beaten

butter, melted, for cooking
pancakes

powdered sugar, sifted,
for dusting

1   Sift the flour and cocoa into a large bowl, mix in the sugar, and make a well in the middle of the mixture. In a small bowl, whisk the milk and egg together, using a hand whisk, and pour into the well. Stir with a wooden spoon to form a smooth batter.

2   Heat a nonstick skillet over medium heat and brush with melted butter. Pour in the batter to make 3½in. rounds. Cook 1 to 2 minutes, or until the top of each pancake begins to show small bubbles, then turn over with a spatula and cook on the second side 30 seconds more. Remove from the pan and repeat until all the pancake batter has been used.

3   Transfer the pancakes to plates, dust with powdered sugar, and serve warm.

Pear clafoutis with chocolate

PREPARATION TIME 25 minutes   COOKING TIME 20–25 minutes

6 tbsp. butter, softened, plus extra for greasing
⅓ cup plus 4 tsp. sugar
2 eggs, lightly beaten
1 cup self-rising flour
¾ cup ground almonds
½ cup milk
3½oz. bittersweet chocolate, melted and left to cool
3 pears, ripe but not soft, peeled, quartered, and cored
light cream, to serve (optional)

1 Preheat the oven to 350°F. Grease a 1½ quart baking dish with butter.

2 In a large bowl, cream the butter and sugar together, using an electric hand mixer, then beat in the eggs, a little at a time. Combine the flour and ground almonds and fold into the butter mixture with the milk and melted chocolate to make a batter. Scatter the pears in the bottom of the baking dish and pour the batter mixture over.

3 Bake in the hot oven 20 to 25 minutes; the middle should still be soft. Remove from the oven and let the clafoutis cool slightly, before serving with cream, if desired.

Mocha creams with ricotta & coffee liqueur

PREPARATION TIME 25 minutes, plus chilling   COOKING TIME 5 minutes

1 cup plus 3 tbsp. heavy
  cream
1¾oz. bittersweet chocolate,
  broken into pieces
12oz. ricotta cheese
¾ cup plus 4 tsp. powdered
  sugar
2 tbsp. coffee liqueur
1 tbsp. coffee beans, freshly
  ground

1 In a small saucepan, heat ½ cup plus 2 tbsp. of the cream over low heat until just simmering, then remove from the heat and add the chocolate. Stir until smooth, using a metal spoon, and pour into a clean bowl to cool.
2 Place the ricotta, powdered sugar, liqueur, and coffee beans in the bowl of a food processor and process until smooth. Add the remaining cream and process briefly until all the ingredients are just combined.
3 Divide the ricotta mixture evenly between 4 glasses. Spoon 1 tbsp. of the chocolate mixture on top of the ricotta mixture in each glass and refrigerate 30 to 40 minutes until just firm.

Chocolate crèmes brûlées

PREPARATION TIME 15 minutes, plus chilling   COOKING TIME 40–45 minutes

2½ cups plus 2 tbsp. heavy cream
2¾oz. bittersweet chocolate, broken into pieces
1 tsp. vanilla extract
6 egg yolks
3 tbsp. sugar
⅓ cup packed light brown sugar

1 Preheat the oven to 250°F.

2 In a small saucepan, heat the cream and chocolate together over low heat until the chocolate is just melted. In a large bowl, beat the vanilla extract, egg yolks, and sugar together, using a hand whisk, then whisk in the heated cream mixture, combining well.

3 Divide the mixture evenly between 4 x 5oz ramekins or other baking dishes. Place the ramekins in a bain marie (see page 10) and bake in the warm oven 35 to 40 minutes, or until the custards are just set.

4 Remove the dish from the oven and take the ramekins out of the dish using tongs, then let cool 30 minutes before refrigerating overnight.

5 Remove from the refrigerator. Sprinkle the brown sugar over the tops of the custards and place under a very hot broiler until the sugar melts and caramelizes (or use a domestic blowtorch). Serve immediately.

Chocolate mud pastries

PREPARATION TIME 20 minutes   COOKING TIME 20–25 minutes

MAKES 12 pastries

13oz. packet ready-rolled
    puff pastry
2¾oz. bittersweet chocolate,
    broken into pieces
2 tbsp. butter, chopped
5 tbsp. superfine sugar
1 egg, lightly beaten
1 tsp. vanilla extract
1 tbsp. all-purpose flour
powdered sugar, sifted,
    for dusting

1   Preheat the oven to 400°F.

2   Cut the pastry into 12 squares of about 4in., which will roughly fit the holes of a 12-hole muffin pan with about ½in. extra. Gently ease each pastry square into a muffin hole without stretching it. Refrigerate while preparing the filling.

3   In a small saucepan, heat the chocolate and butter over low heat and stir until just melted. Remove from the heat and set aside to cool 10 minutes, then stir in the sugar, egg, vanilla extract, and flour. Spoon 1 to 2 tbsp. of the chocolate mixture into the middle of each pastry cup, taking care not to overfill.

4   Bake in the hot oven 15 to 20 minutes, or until the pastry is golden and the filling has puffed up. Remove from the oven and leave the pastries in the pans 5 minutes, then transfer to a wire rack to cool completely. Dust the pastries with powdered sugar.

Chocolate self-saucing pudding

PREPARATION TIME 15 minutes   COOKING TIME 20–25 minutes

6 tbsp. butter, plus extra
    for greasing
1 cup plus 3 tbsp. self-rising
    flour
2 tbsp. unsweetened cocoa
    powder
⅓ cup plus 4 tsp. sugar
½ cup milk
1 tsp. vanilla extract
1 egg, lightly beaten

For the topping
½ cup packed light brown
    sugar
2 tbsp. unsweetened cocoa
    powder

1 Preheat the oven to 350°F. Grease a 1½ quart baking dish with butter.

2 In a medium-sized bowl, combine the flour, cocoa, and sugar. In a small saucepan, heat the butter, milk, and vanilla extract over low heat until the butter has just melted, then set aside to cool 5 minutes. Whisk in the egg, using a hand whisk, then stir all of the liquid ingredients into the dry ingredients to combine. Pour the mixture into the prepared ovenproof dish.

3 For the topping, combine the brown sugar with the cocoa in a bowl, then sprinkle over the chocolate mixture in the dish. Pour over 1¼ cups boiling water. Bake in the hot oven 15 to 20 minutes, or until the pudding is firm but still slightly soft in the middle.

4 Remove from the oven and let cool 5 minutes before serving.

Steamed chocolate pudding

PREPARATION TIME 20 minutes   COOKING TIME 1¾ hours

SERVES 4–6

7 tbsp. butter, softened, plus extra for greasing

⅓ cup plus 4 tsp. sugar

2 eggs, lightly beaten

¾ cup plus 1 tbsp. self-rising flour

2 tbsp. unsweetened cocoa powder

3½ oz. bittersweet chocolate, melted

2 tbsp. milk

1 recipe quantity Rich Chocolate Sauce (see page 188) or Espresso Chocolate Sauce (see page 191)

1 Grease a 1½ quart pudding basin or heatproof round bowl with butter. In a large bowl, beat the butter and sugar together until light and creamy, using an electric hand mixer, then add the eggs a little at a time until smooth. Sift the flour and cocoa together and fold into the mixture with the chocolate and milk.

2 Spoon into the prepared basin and cover with a double layer of foil secured with string. Place the basin in a large saucepan and fill with water to come halfway up the side of the basin. Bring the water to a boil, turn down to a simmer, and steam the pudding 1¾ hours, adding extra boiling water as required.

3 Remove the basin from the saucepan and let cool 10 minutes, then turn the pudding out onto a serving plate. Serve with one of the chocolate sauces.

Chocolate croissant bread pudding

PREPARATION TIME 15 minutes   COOKING TIME 40–45 minutes

6 mini or 3 large chocolate
    croissants
5 eggs
1 tsp. vanilla extract
⅓ cup plus 4 tsp. sugar
6½ cups milk
light cream, for serving
    (optional)

1   Preheat the oven to 300°F. Cut the chocolate croissants into slices about ¼in. thick and place them in the bottom of a 2-quart baking dish about 9in. in diameter.

2   In a large bowl, beat together the eggs, vanilla extract, and sugar, using a hand whisk. Then whisk in the milk.

3   Place the dish in a bain marie (see page 10) and bake in the warm oven 40 to 45 minutes, or until the sides are firm but the middle is still slightly wobbly.

4   Remove the dish from the oven and let cool 5 minutes before serving with cream, if desired.

Chocolate & raspberry tart

PREPARATION TIME 20 minutes   COOKING TIME 35–40 minutes

MAKES 1 x 9in. tart

1 x 9in. Sweet Shortcrust
   Pastry shell, baked (see
   page 15)
5½oz. bittersweet chocolate,
   broken into pieces
⅓ cup heavy cream
6 tbsp. butter, chopped
2 eggs
3 tbsp. plus 3 tsp. superfine
   sugar
1 tbsp. light corn syrup
1 cup raspberries, plus extra
   for serving (optional)
powdered sugar, for dusting
1 recipe quantity Chocolate
   Marsala Cream (see
   page 193)

1   Preheat the oven to 300°F. Place the baked pastry shell on a baking sheet.

2   In a small saucepan, melt the chocolate, cream, and butter together over low heat, then remove the pan from the heat and set aside to cool. In a large bowl, beat the eggs, sugar, and light corn syrup together for a few minutes until pale and light, using an electric hand mixer. Stir in the chocolate mixture, using a wooden spoon. Scatter the raspberries over the bottom of the tart and pour the chocolate filling on top, taking care not to overfill.

3   Bake in the warm oven 35 to 40 minutes, or until the middle of the tart is just set. Remove from the oven and let cool completely on the baking sheet.

4   Dust the tart with powdered sugar just before serving and serve with extra raspberries, if desired, and the chocolate Marsala cream.

Tangy lemon & chocolate tarts

PREPARATION TIME 35 minutes   COOKING TIME 17–20 minutes

MAKES 4 x 4in. tarts

4 x 4in. Sweet Shortcrust Pastry shells, baked (see page 15)

juice and finely grated zest of 3 lemons

⅔ cup plus 1½ tsp. superfine sugar

5 eggs, lightly beaten

1 stick plus 3 tbsp. butter, chopped

3½oz. bittersweet chocolate, melted, plus shards to decorate

unsweetened cocoa powder, sifted, for dusting

1   Preheat the oven to 350°F. Place the baked pastry shells on a baking sheet.

2   Place the lemon juice and zest, the sugar, eggs, and butter in the top of a double boiler and heat, stirring constantly with a wooden spoon, about 15 minutes until the mixture thickens and coats the back of the spoon. Remove from the heat and stir in the melted chocolate. Pour the mixture into the baked pastry shells, filling them about two-thirds full.

3   Bake in the hot oven 12 to 15 minutes, or until the custard is just firm, then remove from the oven and let the tarts cool completely on the sheet. Place a shard of chocolate on each tart and dust with cocoa just before serving.

White chocolate & berry tarts

PREPARATION TIME 30 minutes   COOKING TIME 8–10 minutes

MAKES 12 tarts

1 stick plus 1 tbsp. butter, melted, plus extra for greasing
8 sheets filo pastry
5 tbsp. superfine sugar
⅔ cup heavy cream, whipped to soft peaks
4½oz. white chocolate, melted and left to cool
1½ cups mixed raspberries and blackberries

1   Preheat the oven to 350°F. Grease a 12-hole muffin pan with butter.

2   Lay a sheet of filo pastry on the work surface and brush with melted butter. Sprinkle over some of the sugar. Place a second layer of pastry on top of the first layer, lightly butter, then sprinkle with sugar. Repeat until all of the layers have been used, finishing with a butter and sugar layer. Cut the pastry stack into 12 squares and ease a square into each hole of the muffin pan.

3   Bake in the hot oven 8 to 10 minutes, or until the pastry is golden brown. Remove from the oven and let the filo cases cool in the pan.

4   For the filling, gently fold the cream and melted chocolate together in a bowl, using a metal spoon. Remove the tart cases from the pan and, just before serving, divide the filling mixture evenly between them and spoon the mixed berries over.

150

DESERT

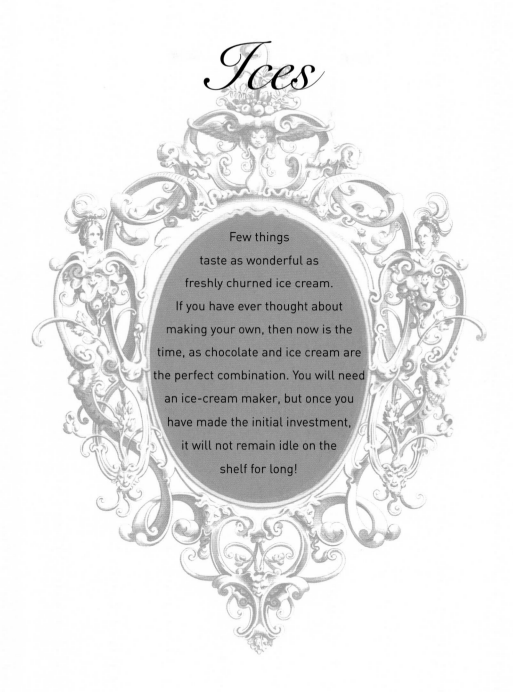

Ices

Few things
taste as wonderful as
freshly churned ice cream.
If you have ever thought about
making your own, then now is the
time, as chocolate and ice cream are
the perfect combination. You will need
an ice-cream maker, but once you
have made the initial investment,
it will not remain idle on the
shelf for long!

Rich chocolate ice cream

PREPARATION TIME 20 minutes, plus chilling and churning   COOKING TIME 5 minutes

MAKES 4⅓ cups

1¼ cups plus 1 tbsp. milk
1¼ cups plus 1 tbsp. heavy
  cream
12oz. bittersweet or milk
  chocolate, broken into
  pieces
4 egg yolks
⅓ cup plus 4 tsp. sugar

1   In a small saucepan, heat the milk, cream, and chocolate together over low heat until the chocolate is just melted. Remove the pan from the heat and stir with a wooden spoon until smooth.

2   In a large bowl, beat the egg yolks and sugar together, using a hand whisk, then pour in the hot chocolate mixture, whisking constantly. Return the mixture to the saucepan and heat, stirring constantly with a wooden spoon, until the mixture just begins to thicken and lightly coats the back of the spoon. Do not allow the mixture to boil or it will curdle.

3   Remove from the heat, pour into a clean bowl, and let cool completely. Refrigerate 3 hours or overnight, then churn in an ice-cream maker according to the manufacturer's instructions.

Strawberry & white chocolate cheesecake ice cream

PREPARATION TIME 15 minutes, plus chilling and churning   MAKES 4⅓ cups

7oz. cream cheese, softened
heaped ⅔ cup sugar
1 cup plus 2 tbsp. heavy
 cream
1 cup plus 2 tbsp. sour cream
1 cup strawberries, chopped
4½oz. white chocolate, melted
 and left to cool

1   In a large bowl, beat the cream cheese and sugar together until soft, using an electric hand mixer. Whisk in the cream and sour cream, then stir in the strawberries and melted chocolate until just combined.

2   Refrigerate 3 hours or overnight, then churn in an ice-cream maker according to the manufacturer's instructions.

Mint chocolate-chip ice cream

PREPARATION TIME 20 minutes, plus chilling and churning   COOKING TIME 5 minutes

MAKES 4⅓ cups

1½ cups plus 2 tbsp. milk
½ cup plus 2 tsp. sugar
1½ cups plus 2 tbsp. heavy
  cream
6oz. bittersweet chocolate,
  grated
2 tsp. peppermint extract
2 to 3 drops green coloring
  (optional)

1   In a medium-sized saucepan, heat the milk and sugar together over medium heat until the sugar dissolves. Pour into a clean bowl and add the cream. Leave the mixture to cool completely before stirring in the chocolate, peppermint extract, and green coloring, if using.

2   Refrigerate 3 hours or overnight, then churn in an ice-cream maker according to the manufacturer's instructions.

Ginger & chocolate ice cream

PREPARATION TIME 25 minutes, plus chilling and churning   COOKING TIME 5 minutes

MAKES 4⅓ cups

1 cup plus 2 tbsp. milk
3½oz. bittersweet chocolate,
    broken into pieces
3 egg yolks
⅓ cup plus 4 tsp. sugar
2 cups plus 2 tbsp. heavy
    cream
3½oz. candied ginger,
    chopped
1 tbsp. light corn syrup

1 In a small saucepan, heat the milk and chocolate together over low heat until just melted.

2 In a large bowl, beat the egg yolks and sugar together, using a hand whisk, then pour in the hot chocolate mixture, whisking constantly. Return the mixture to the saucepan and heat, stirring constantly with a wooden spoon, until the mixture just begins to thicken and lightly coats the back of the spoon. Do not allow the mixture to boil or it will curdle.

3 Remove from the heat, pour into a clean bowl, and let cool completely, then stir in the cream, ginger, and corn syrup. Refrigerate 3 hours or overnight, then churn in an ice-cream maker according to the manufacturer's instructions.

Chocolate sorbet

PREPARATION TIME 30 minutes, plus chilling and churning   COOKING TIME 25 minutes

MAKES 4⅓ cups

1 cup plus 4 tsp. sugar
1 cup plus 3 tbsp. unsweetened
  cocoa powder, sifted
2 tsp. vanilla extract

1 In a large saucepan, mix together the sugar and 3¾ cups water over medium heat, stirring well until the sugar dissolves. Whisk in the cocoa, using a hand whisk. Bring to a boil, then reduce the heat and simmer 20 minutes over low heat, stirring occasionally. Remove from the heat, pour into a clean bowl, and add the vanilla extract, then let cool completely.

2 Refrigerate 2 hours or overnight, then churn in an ice-cream maker according to the manufacturer's instructions.

White chocolate & raspberry parfait

PREPARATION TIME 25 minutes, plus freezing   COOKING TIME 5 minutes

½ cup heavy cream
4½oz. white chocolate,
   broken into pieces
2 egg whites
⅓ cup plus 4 tsp. sugar
1 cup raspberries, lightly
   crushed, plus extra, whole,
   for serving
1 tbsp. strawberry or
   raspberry liqueur

1   In a small saucepan, heat the cream and chocolate together over low heat until just melted, then set aside to cool. In a large bowl, whisk the egg whites until soft peaks form, using an electric hand mixer, then gradually add the sugar until the mixture is thick and shiny. Fold in the chocolate cream, raspberries, and liqueur and divide evenly between 4 freezerproof ¾-cup molds. Freeze the parfaits 3 hours or overnight.

2   Remove the parfaits from the freezer, turn out onto individual plates, and serve with the extra raspberries.

Broiled pineapple, macadamia & chocolate sundaes

PREPARATION TIME 15 minutes   COOKING TIME 5 minutes

1 small, ripe pineapple, peeled
⅓ cup plus 2 tsp. packed light brown sugar
2 tbsp. dark rum
8 scoops Rich Chocolate Ice Cream (see page 146) or good-quality store-bought ice cream, slightly softened
1 recipe quantity Chocolate Rum Sauce (see page 191)
½ cup macadamia nuts, roasted and chopped
4 ice-cream wafers (optional)

1 Cut the pineapple into quarters and remove the core, then slice into ½in. slices. Place the slices in a large bowl with the brown sugar and dark rum and toss until well combined.

2 Place the pineapple slices on a broiler pan under a hot broiler and broil a few minutes until the pineapple has warmed slightly and has a light glaze.

3 Divide the broiled pineapple slices between 4 plates and top each one with 2 scoops of chocolate ice cream and the chocolate rum sauce. Sprinkle with chopped macadamia nuts and serve with ice-cream wafers, if using.

Peach & amaretto sundae with chocolate

PREPARATION TIME 30 minutes, plus cooling   COOKING TIME 15–17 minutes

⅔ cup sugar

4 ripe, firm, yellow peaches

8 scoops Rich Chocolate Ice Cream (see page 146) or good-quality bought ice cream, slightly softened

1 recipe quantity Rich Chocolate Sauce (see page 188)

½ cup crushed amaretto cookies

1   In a small saucepan, heat the sugar and 1 cup water together over medium heat until the sugar dissolves, stirring frequently with a metal spoon. Bring to a simmer, then add the peaches and cook 8 to 10 minutes until just tender. Remove the peaches from the syrup using a slotted spoon and set aside in a bowl to cool completely, then peel, cut in half horizontally, and remove the pits.

2   Return the syrup to the heat and bring to a boil, then reduce the heat and simmer until the syrup is reduced by half. Pour into a bowl and let cool.

3   Divide the peach halves equally between 4 dishes and spoon over some of the syrup. Place a scoop of chocolate ice cream on each peach half, top with some rich chocolate sauce, and sprinkle with the crushed amaretto cookies.

Frozen chocolate yogurt

PREPARATION TIME 20 minutes, plus chilling and churning   COOKING TIME 5 minutes

MAKES 4⅓ cups

⅓ cup plus 4 tsp. sugar
1 tbsp. cornstarch
1½ cups plus 2 tbsp. milk
1 egg, lightly beaten
½ cup chocolate sauce
1 tbsp. honey
1½ cups plus 2 tbsp. plain or
  vanilla-flavored yogurt
1 tsp. vanilla extract

1 In a small bowl, mix the sugar and cornstarch to a paste, using a little of the milk. Place the remaining milk in a small saucepan over low heat and, using a hand whisk, whisk in the cornstarch mixture and the egg. Continue to heat, stirring constantly with a wooden spoon, until the mixture thickens and coats the back of the spoon. Pour the mixture into a clean bowl and stir in the chocolate syrup and honey. Set aside until cold, then refrigerate 3 hours.

2 Whisk in the yogurt and vanilla extract, using a hand whisk, then churn in an ice-cream maker according to the manufacturer's instructions.

Chocolate treats & drinks

Handmade chocolates and truffles are ideal for that extra-special occasion, and make beautiful gifts for friends and family. Chocolate drinks—from comforting Hot Chocolate to warm up a cold winter's night, to a divine Iced Mocha Shake for hot summer days—are the perfect indulgent treat.

Cranberry & port chocolate truffles

PREPARATION TIME 25 minutes, plus chilling   COOKING TIME 5 minutes

MAKES 30 truffles

7oz. bittersweet chocolate, broken into pieces
¼ cup heavy cream
2 tbsp. port
¼ cup dried cranberries, chopped
9oz. white chocolate, melted and left to cool

1   In a small saucepan, combine the chocolate and cream over low heat until the chocolate is just melted, stirring frequently with a wooden spoon. Remove from the heat and stir until smooth, then add the port and dried cranberries. Pour into a clean bowl and let cool completely, then refrigerate about 30 minutes until firm.

2   Roll teaspoonfuls of the mixture in the melted white chocolate to form balls, put on a baking sheet lined with wax paper and refrigerate 1 hour until firm.

White chocolate, citrus & coconut truffles

PREPARATION TIME 25 minutes, plus chilling COOKING TIME 5 minutes

MAKES 30 truffles

scant ½ cup coconut cream

12oz. white chocolate, broken into pieces

2 tsp. lemon zest, finely grated

2 tsp. lime zest, finely grated

2 tbsp. coconut rum liqueur

1 cup flaked coconut

1 In a small saucepan, combine the coconut cream and chocolate together over a low heat until just melted, stirring frequently with a wooden spoon. Remove from the heat and stir until smooth. Pour into a clean bowl and let cool, then stir in the lemon and lime zests and liqueur. Refrigerate about 30 minutes until firm.

2 Roll teaspoonfuls of the mixture in the flaked coconut to form balls. Place on a baking sheet lined with wax paper and refrigerate 1 hour until firm.

Peanut butter & milk chocolate truffles

PREPARATION TIME 30 minutes, plus chilling   COOKING TIME 5 minutes   MAKES 30 truffles

7oz. milk chocolate, broken
    into pieces
scant ½ cup heavy cream
3 tbsp. crunchy peanut butter
scant ⅔ cup roasted peanuts,
    crushed

1   In a small saucepan, combine the chocolate and cream over low heat until the chocolate is just melted, stirring frequently with a wooden spoon. Remove from the heat, add the peanut butter, and stir until smooth. Pour into a clean bowl and let cool completely, then refrigerate about 30 minutes until firm.

2   Roll rounded teaspoonfuls of the mixture in the crushed peanuts, then place on a baking sheet lined with wax paper and refrigerate 1 hour until firm.

Double chocolate truffles

PREPARATION TIME 25 minutes, plus chilling   COOKING TIME 5 minutes   MAKES 20 truffles

5½oz. bittersweet chocolate,
    broken into pieces
¼ cup heavy cream
2 tbsp. liqueur of your
    choice (e.g. Kahlua,
    Grand Marnier)
2 tbsp. unsweetened cocoa
    powder, sifted

1   In a small saucepan, combine the chocolate and cream over low heat until the chocolate is just melted, stirring frequently with a wooden spoon. Remove from the heat and add the liqueur. Pour the mixture into a clean bowl and let cool completely, then refrigerate about 30 minutes until firm.

2   Roll teaspoonfuls of the mixture into small balls and toss in the cocoa to coat. Place the balls on a baking sheet lined with wax paper and refrigerate 1 hour until firm.

Chocolate & orange truffles

PREPARATION TIME 20 minutes, plus chilling   COOKING TIME 5 minutes   MAKES 18 truffles

5½oz. bittersweet chocolate, broken into pieces
¼ cup heavy cream
3 tbsp. orange liqueur
zest of 1 orange, finely grated
3 tbsp. orange liqueur
zest of 1 orange, finely grated
powdered sugar, sifted, for coating
3 tbsp. orange liqueur
zest of 1 orange, finely grated
powdered sugar, sifted, for coating

1 In a small saucepan, combine the chocolate and cream over low heat until the chocolate is just melted, stirring frequently with a wooden spoon. Remove from the heat and stir in the liqueur and orange zest, using a wooden spoon. Pour into a clean bowl and let cool completely, then refrigerate about 30 minutes until firm.

2 Roll teaspoonfuls of the mixture into balls and coat with powdered sugar. Place on a baking sheet lined with wax paper and refrigerate 1 hour until firm.

Gingernut & chocolate truffles

PREPARATION TIME 25 minutes, plus chilling   COOKING TIME 5 minutes   MAKES 30 truffles

10½oz. ginger snaps, finely crushed
3 tbsp. unsweetened cocoa powder
2 pieces preserved ginger, finely chopped
generous 1 cup sweetened condensed milk
1 cup flaked coconut

1 In a large bowl, mix together the ginger snaps, cocoa, ginger, and sweetened condensed milk until well combined.

2 Using slightly wet hands, roll rounded teaspoonfuls of the mixture into balls and roll in the coconut to coat. Place on a baking sheet lined with wax paper and refrigerate 1 hour until firm.

Roasted almond drops (right)

PREPARATION TIME 15 minutes, plus chilling   COOKING TIME 5 minutes

MAKES 18 drops

7oz. bittersweet or milk chocolate, broken into pieces

2 cups slivered almonds, toasted

1   In a small saucepan, melt the chocolate over low heat, stirring until smooth. Remove from the heat and stir in the toasted almonds until well combined.

2   Let cool 5 minutes, then place teaspoonfuls of the mixture on a baking sheet lined with wax paper and refrigerate about 30 minutes until firm.

Roasted macadamia & ginger white chocolate drops

PREPARATION TIME 15 minutes, plus chilling   COOKING TIME 5 minutes   MAKES 18 drops

7oz. white chocolate, broken into pieces

1 cup whole macadamia nuts, roasted

3 pieces preserved ginger, finely chopped

1   In a small saucepan, melt the chocolate over low heat, stirring until smooth. Add the nuts and ginger, and stir to combine, using a wooden spoon.

2   Place teaspoonfuls of the mixture on a baking sheet lined with wax paper to create neat drops, then refrigerate about 30 minutes until firm.

Mint chocolate fudge

PREPARATION TIME 30 minutes, plus chilling   COOKING TIME 5 minutes

MAKES 16 squares

12oz. bittersweet chocolate, broken into pieces
1 x 14oz. can sweetened condensed milk
scant 1½ cups powdered sugar
2 tsp. vanilla extract
1 tbsp. peppermint extract

1 Line a shallow 9in. square cake pan with baking paper.
2 In a small saucepan, combine the chocolate and sweetened condensed milk over low heat until just melted. Remove from the heat and stir until smooth, using a wooden spoon, then stir in the sugar and both extracts.
3 Pour the fudge mixture into the prepared pan and let cool completely, then refrigerate about 30 minutes until firm. Turn out of the pan, using the paper to help you, before cutting the fudge into squares, using a sharp knife.

Cappuccino slims

PREPARATION TIME 15 minutes, plus chilling   COOKING TIME 5 minutes

MAKES 16 squares

7oz. bittersweet chocolate,
  broken into pieces
1 tsp. instant coffee powder
1 tbsp. coffee liqueur
5½oz. white chocolate, broken
  into pieces
2 tsp. unsweetened cocoa
  powder, sifted

1 Line a shallow 9in. square cake pan with baking paper, letting the edges hang over the sides of the pan.

2 In a small saucepan, heat the bittersweet chocolate over low heat until just melted, then remove from the heat and stir until smooth, using a wooden spoon. Stir in the coffee and liqueur. Spread the mixture over the base of the prepared pan, using a palette knife, and refrigerate about 30 minutes until firm.

3 In a small saucepan, heat the white chocolate over low heat until melted, then spread it over the bittersweet chocolate mixture using a palette knife. Dust the top with cocoa.

4 Refrigerate 30 minutes, then remove from the refrigerator and turn out from the pan, using the paper to help you, before cutting into squares with a knife that has been dipped in hot water first to warm it.

Chocolate-dipped dried fruits

PREPARATION TIME 15 minutes, plus chilling   COOKING TIME 5 minutes

MAKES 24 chocolates

9oz. bittersweet chocolate,
    broken into pieces
24 pieces dried fruit,
    including apricots,
    pear, and pineapple

1   In a small saucepan, heat the chocolate over low heat until just melted, then remove from the heat and stir until smooth.

2   Wipe the dried fruit with paper towel and dip each piece in the melted chocolate to cover halfway. (If the chocolate runs off without making a nice coating, let it cool a few minutes, then try again.)

3   Place the dipped fruit on a baking sheet lined with wax paper and refrigerate about 30 minutes until the chocolate has set.

Chocolate florentines

PREPARATION TIME 35 minutes   COOKING TIME 6–8 minutes

MAKES 24 florentines

½ stick butter, plus extra for greasing
3 tbsp. plus 1 tsp. superfine sugar
2 tsp. honey
½ cup sliced almonds
¼ cup red candied cherries, chopped
heaped ⅓ cup golden raisins
5½oz. milk chocolate, melted and cooled

1 Preheat the oven to 350ºF. Line 2 large baking sheets with baking paper.

2 In a small saucepan, melt the butter, sugar, and honey together over low heat until melted. Remove the pan from the heat. In a large bowl, mix together the almonds, candied cherries, and golden raisins, then pour the butter mixture into the bowl, stirring well with a wooden spoon to combine. Place tablespoonfuls of the mixture on the baking sheet, leaving 2in. between them for room to spread, and press down lightly to flatten the mixture into rounds.

3 Bake in the hot oven 6 to 8 minutes, or until lightly golden. Remove the baking sheets from the oven, let the florentines cool 5 minutes, then transfer them to a wire rack to cool completely.

4 When cold, turn the florentines over (the backs will be smooth) and spread with melted chocolate. Once the chocolate has cooled slightly, make lines using a fork or wavy icing spreader. Leave on the baking sheets until the chocolate sets.

Chocolate ginger snap squares

PREPARATION TIME 25 minutes, plus chilling COOKING TIME 5 minutes

MAKES 16 squares

14oz. bittersweet chocolate, broken into pieces

1 stick plus 1 tbsp. butter, chopped

1 x 14oz. can sweetened condensed milk

5 pieces preserved ginger, finely chopped

9oz. ginger snaps, crushed

¾ cup flaked coconut, toasted, plus 3 tbsp. for sprinkling

1 Line a shallow 9in. square cake pan with kitchen foil, leaving enough at the edges to hang over the sides.

2 In a small saucepan, heat the chocolate and butter together until just melted, then remove from the heat and stir until smooth. Stir in the remaining ingredients and spoon into the prepared pan. Sprinkle with the extra coconut.

3 Refrigerate the chocolate ginger snap mixture until firm. Remove from the refrigerator and turn out of the pan, using the foil to help you, then cut into squares with a sharp knife.

Chocolate & almond truffle squares

PREPARATION TIME 25 minutes, plus chilling   COOKING TIME 5 minutes   MAKES 16 squares

1lb. bittersweet chocolate, broken into pieces
½ cup heavy cream
3 tbsp. amaretto liqueur
⅓ cup roasted almonds, roughly chopped

1   Line a shallow 8in. square cake pan with foil.

2   In a small saucepan, heat 12oz. of the chocolate with the cream over a low heat until just melted. Remove the pan from the heat and stir until smooth, using a wooden spoon. Stir in the amaretto, then set the mixture aside.

3   In a clean pan, melt the remaining chocolate separately over low heat. Spread half of the melted chocolate over the bottom of the prepared pan.

4   Refrigerate the pan until the chocolate is firm, then top with the truffle mixture and sprinkle with the chopped almonds. Drizzle the remaining melted chocolate over the truffle mixture in a decorative pattern. Refrigerate about 30 minutes until firm, then turn out using the foil to help you, before cutting into squares, using a sharp knife.

Best-ever hot chocolate

PREPARATION TIME 15 minutes   COOKING TIME 5 minutes

1 cup plus 2 tbsp. milk
1 cup plus 2 tbsp. heavy
  cream
2 tbsp. superfine sugar
4½oz. bittersweet chocolate,
  broken into pieces
unsweetened cocoa powder,
  sifted for dusting (optional)

1 Heat the milk and half the cream in a saucepan until just boiling. Remove from the heat and beat in the sugar and chocolate, using an electric hand mixer.

2 Divide the chocolate milk equally between 4 small cups (the mixture is very rich). Whip the remaining cream until it forms soft peaks, using an electric hand mixer, then place a tablespoonful on each cup and dust with unsweetened cocoa powder, if using. Serve immediately.

Nutty chocolate coffee

PREPARATION TIME 5 minutes   COOKING TIME 5 minutes

1 quart plus ⅓ cup milk
4 tsp. unsweetened cocoa
   powder
4 tsp. instant coffee powder
¼ cup superfine sugar
¼ cup hazelnut liqueur
½ cup heavy cream, whipped
   to soft peaks
pinch cinnamon, to sprinkle

1 In a medium-sized saucepan, heat the milk until just boiling. Remove from the heat and whisk in the cocoa, coffee, sugar, and liqueur.

2 Strain the mixture into a clean saucepan and divide equally between 4 cups. Top each cup with a tablespoonful of the whipped cream, then sprinkle over the cinnamon.

Chocolate Irish coffee

PREPARATION TIME 10 minutes

3 tbsp. unsweetened cocoa
   powder
3¾ cups freshly brewed coffee
4 tsp. superfine sugar
2 tbsp. Irish whisky
¼ cup Chocolate Chantilly
   Cream (see page 194)
3 tbsp. grated bittersweet
   chocolate

1 Place the cocoa in a bowl and blend to a paste with ½ cup of the coffee. Whisk in the remaining coffee, the sugar, and whisky, using a hand whisk.

2 Divide the coffee mixture evenly between 4 heatproof glasses or mugs. Top each one with a tablespoonful of chocolate Chantilly cream, then sprinkle with the grated bittersweet chocolate.

Iced mocha shake

PREPARATION TIME 20 minutes, plus chilling

3¾ cups hot, strong coffee

3 tbsp. unsweetened cocoa powder

2 tbsp. superfine sugar

4 scoops Rich Chocolate Ice Cream (see page 146) or good-quality store-bought ice cream

½ cup heavy cream, whipped to soft peaks

¼ cup grated bittersweet chocolate

1 Pour the coffee into a large bowl. In a small bowl, mix the cocoa to a paste with 2 tablespoonfuls of the coffee. Whisk the paste back into the remaining coffee, with the sugar, using a hand whisk, then stir well with a wooden spoon until the sugar dissolves. Let cool completely, then refrigerate 30 minutes.

2 Place a scoop of chocolate ice cream in the bottom of each of 4 tall glasses. Pour the coffee over, dividing it equally between the glasses. Spoon a generous tablespoonful of the whipped cream over the top of each glass, then sprinkle with grated chocolate. Serve immediately.

Divine iced mint chocolate (right)

PREPARATION TIME 5 minutes

2¾oz. bittersweet or milk
    chocolate, melted and left
    to cool
1¾ cups cold milk
scant ⅔ cup natural or vanilla-
    flavored yogurt
6 mint leaves, plus extra to
    decorate
4 scoops Rich Chocolate Ice
    Cream (see page 146) or
    good-quality

1 Place the chocolate, milk, yogurt, and mint in a
blender; blend until smooth.
2 Divide the milk mixture equally between 4 tall glasses
and top with a scoop of chocolate ice cream. Decorate
with mint leaves and serve immediately.

Chocolate milkshakes

PREPARATION TIME 5 minutes

2 cups cold milk
1 tsp. vanilla extract
¼ cup chocolate sauce
8 tbsp. Rich Chocolate Ice
    Cream (see page 146) or
    good-quality store-bought
    ice cream

1 Combine all of the ingredients in a blender and
process until well combined.
2 Divide the milkshake mixture equally between 4 glasses.

Sauces, icings & frostings

These recipes deserve a chapter devoted just to them as you will use them time and time again. While a number of the recipes throughout the book suggest a sauce, frosting or icing, feel free to mix and match. All of the recipes are simple to make and will transform a favorite dessert into something special.

Rich chocolate sauce (right)

PREPARATION TIME 10 minutes   COOKING TIME 5 minutes

MAKES 1½ cups

1 cup plus 2 tbsp. heavy
   cream
5½oz. bittersweet chocolate,
   broken into pieces
1 tbsp. chocolate liqueur
   (optional)
1 tbsp. powdered sugar
1 tsp. vanilla extract

1 In a small saucepan, combine the cream and chocolate over low heat, stirring with a wooden spoon until smooth. Remove the pan from the heat.

2 Stir in the liqueur, if using, sugar, and vanilla extract. Serve warm.

White chocolate sauce

PREPARATION TIME 10 minutes   COOKING TIME 5 minutes

MAKES 1½ cups

1 cup plus 2 tbsp. heavy
   cream
4½oz. white chocolate, broken
   into pieces
1 tsp. vanilla extract

1 In a small saucepan, combine the cream and chocolate over low heat until the chocolate melts. Add the vanilla extract and stir until smooth, using a wooden spoon.

2 Remove the pan from the heat and serve warm.

Chocolate rum sauce

PREPARATION TIME 10 minutes   COOKING TIME 5 minutes

MAKES 1¼ cups

1 cup plus 2 tbsp. heavy
  cream
2 tsp. sugar
3½oz. bittersweet chocolate,
  broken into pieces
2 tbsp. dark rum

1 In a small saucepan, heat the cream, sugar, and chocolate together over a low heat until the chocolate melts, stirring with a wooden spoon until smooth.
2 Remove the pan from the heat, stir in the rum, and serve warm.

Espresso chocolate sauce (left)

PREPARATION TIME 10 minutes   COOKING TIME 5 minutes

MAKES 1½ cups

1 cup plus 2 tbsp. heavy
  cream
5½oz. bittersweet chocolate,
  broken into pieces
¼ cup hot, strong espresso
  coffee
1 tbsp. coffee liqueur

1 In a small saucepan, combine the cream and chocolate over low heat until the chocolate melts. Remove the pan from the heat.
2 Add the coffee and liqueur and set aside to cool 10 minutes before serving.

Chocolate Marsala cream (left)

PREPARATION TIME 10 minutes   MAKES 1 cup

1 cup plus 2 tbsp. heavy
  cream
1 tbsp. powdered sugar
1 tbsp. Marsala wine
unsweetened cocoa powder,
  sifted, to dust

1 In a large bowl, combine the cream, powdered sugar, and Marsala wine and whip to soft peaks, using an electric hand mixer.

2 Dust the top of the cream with cocoa just before serving.

Chocolate mascarpone cream

PREPARATION TIME 10 minutes, plus chilling   MAKES 1 cup

4½oz. milk chocolate, melted
  and left to cool
1 tsp. vanilla extract
4oz. mascarpone cheese

1 In a large bowl, whisk all the ingredients together, using an electric hand mixer.

2 Refrigerate 30 minutes before using.

Chocolate Chantilly cream

PREPARATION TIME 15 minutes   MAKES 1 cup

1 cup plus 2 tbsp. heavy
   cream
2 tbsp. powdered sugar
3½oz. dark or milk chocolate,
   melted and left to cool

1   In a large bowl, whip the cream and powdered sugar together to form soft peaks, using an electric hand mixer.
2   Gently fold in the melted chocolate until just combined, before using.

Chocolate buttercream

PREPARATION TIME 15 minutes, plus chilling   MAKES 1½ cups

1½ sticks butter
1 cup plus 1 tbsp. packed light
   brown sugar
1 egg yolk
1 tbsp. milk
1 tbsp. unsweetened cocoa
   powder
3½oz. bittersweet chocolate,
   melted and left to cool

1   In a large bowl, beat the butter and sugar together until light and fluffy, using an electric hand mixer. Add the remaining ingredients and continue beating until thick and light.
2   Refrigerate 30 minutes before using.

Mocha buttercream

PREPARATION TIME 45 minutes, plus cooling and chilling   COOKING TIME 5 minutes

MAKES 2 cups

¾ cup milk
3½oz. bittersweet chocolate,
  broken into pieces
4 tsp. instant coffee granules
1 tsp. vanilla extract
3 egg yolks
7 tbsp. butter, softened
½ cup plus 2 tbsp. powdered
  sugar

1 In a large saucepan, combine the milk, chocolate, coffee, and vanilla extract over low heat until the chocolate melts, then remove the pan from the heat. Beat the yolks in a bowl and whisk in the chocolate mixture. Return the mixture to the pan and cook, stirring constantly with a wooden spoon, until the mixture begins to thicken and coats the back of the spoon. Do not allow to boil. Pour the mixture into a bowl and set aside to cool 30 minutes.

2 In a clean bowl, whisk the butter until light and creamy, using an electric hand mixer, then add the chocolate mixture with the powdered sugar. Continue to whisk until thick and glossy. Refrigerate 30 minutes before using.

Dark chocolate ganache (right)

PREPARATION TIME 5 minutes, plus cooling   COOKING TIME 5 minutes

MAKES 1 cup

6oz. bittersweet chocolate,
   broken into pieces
2 tbsp. butter
½ cup heavy cream

1   In a small saucepan, combine all of the ingredients over low heat and stir until the chocolate and butter melt. Remove the pan from the heat.

2   Pour into a clean bowl and let cool about 20 minutes, or until the mixture begins to thicken. Use as a filling or topping for your chosen cake recipe or serve warm as a sauce.

White chocolate ganache

PREPARATION TIME 10 minutes, plus cooling   COOKING TIME 5 minutes

MAKES 1 cup

½ cup crème fraîche
4½oz. white chocolate, broken
   into pieces

1   In a small saucepan, heat the crème fraîche over low heat. Remove the pan from the heat and add the white chocolate. Stir gently until the chocolate melts, using a wooden spoon, then continue stirring for a few more minutes until smooth.

2   Set aside to cool 30 minutes, or until the ganache has thickened slightly.

Chocolate cream cheese frosting (left)

PREPARATION TIME 10 minutes   MAKES 1½ cups

9oz. cream cheese, softened
3½oz. bittersweet chocolate,
  melted and left to cool
1 tbsp. butter, softened
1 tsp. vanilla extract
2 cups powdered sugar, sifted

1 In a large bowl, beat the cream cheese until light, using an electric hand mixer.
2 Add the melted chocolate, butter, vanilla extract, and powdered sugar and continue beating until creamy and thickened.

Chocolate rum frosting

PREPARATION TIME 15 minutes   MAKES 1½ cups

3½oz. bittersweet chocolate,
  broken into pieces
2 tbsp. butter, chopped
2⅓ cups powdered sugar
scant ½ cup heavy cream
2 tbsp. dark or light rum
1 tsp. vanilla extract

1 In a small saucepan, combine the chocolate and butter together over low heat and stir until smooth.
2 Place the powdered sugar in a large bowl and, using a wooden spoon, mix in the chocolate mixture, cream, rum, and vanilla extract. Whisk until thick, using an electric hand mixer.

Chocolate fudge frosting

PREPARATION TIME 15 minutes   COOKING TIME 5 minutes

MAKES 1½ cups

2¾oz. bittersweet chocolate, broken into pieces

6 tbsp. butter, chopped

2 cups powdered sugar

2 tbsp. unsweetened cocoa powder

5 tbsp. milk

1 tsp. vanilla extract

1   In a small saucepan, heat the chocolate and butter over low heat until just melted. In a medium-sized bowl, mix the powdered sugar and cocoa together and pour the melted chocolate over. Add the milk and vanilla extract and stir to combine well.

2   Put the bowl containing the mixture into a larger bowl containing a little iced water and beat the mixture with a wooden spoon until it is thick enough to spread and hold its shape.

White chocolate frosting

PREPARATION TIME 10 minutes, plus cooling and chilling   COOKING TIME 5 minutes
MAKES 1½ cups

3½oz. white chocolate,
   broken into pieces
1 cup plus 2 tbsp. heavy
   cream
9oz. mascarpone cheese

1 In a small saucepan, combine the chocolate and
a scant ⅔ cup of the cream over low heat until the
chocolate melts. Remove the pan from the heat and stir
until smooth. Pour the mixture into a clean bowl and let
cool 30 minutes, stirring occasionally, then refrigerate
about 1 hour.

2 In a large bowl, stir the mascarpone until smooth,
using a wooden spoon. Add the chocolate mixture and
as much of the remaining cream as required to make a
spreadable consistency.

Shiny chocolate icing (right)

PREPARATION TIME 15 minutes   MAKES 1 cup

scant 3¼ cups powdered
 sugar
2 tbsp. unsweetened cocoa
 powder
1 tbsp. butter, softened

1 Place the powdered sugar and cocoa in a bowl and make a small well in the middle. Place the butter in the well and add 2½ tbsp. boiling water. Stir until the butter melts, then continue stirring until the icing reaches a spreadable consistency, adding about another 2½ tbsp. water as required. Use immediately.

Creamy chocolate icing

PREPARATION TIME 10 minutes   MAKES 1 cup

scant 1⅔ cups powdered
 sugar
3 tbsp. unsweetened cocoa
 powder
2 tbsp. butter, melted
4 to 5 tbsp. milk

1 Sift the powdered sugar and cocoa into a bowl.
2 Stir in the butter and enough of the milk to make a creamy consistency.

Index

Notes